Screenda
to

Screendance
from Film to Festival

Celebration and Curatorial Practice

CARA HAGAN

McFarland & Company, Inc., Publishers

Jefferson, North Carolina

This book has undergone peer review.

Library of Congress Cataloguing-in-Publication Data

Names: Hagan, Cara, author.
Title: Screendance from film to festival : celebration and curatorial practice / Cara Hagan.
Description: Jefferson, North Carolina : McFarland & Company, Inc., Publishers, 2022. | Includes bibliographical references and index.
Identifiers: LCCN 2022001653 | ISBN 9781476669847 (paperback : acid free paper) ∞ ISBN 9781476645452 (ebook)
Subjects: LCSH: Dance in motion pictures, television, etc. | Choreography. | Film festivals. | Movies by movers (American Dance Festival) | BISAC: PERFORMING ARTS / Dance / General | PERFORMING ARTS / Film / General
Classification: LCC GV1779 .H34 2022 | DDC 793.3—dc23
LC record available at https://lccn.loc.gov/2022001653

British Library cataloguing data are available

ISBN (print) 978-1-4766-6984-7
ISBN (ebook) 978-1-4766-4545-2

Front cover image courtesy of Kitty McNamee

Printed in the United States of America

McFarland & Company, Inc., Publishers
Box 611, Jefferson, North Carolina 28640
www.mcfarlandpub.com

Acknowledgments

I would like to acknowledge that this work was largely written on Cherokee land and that the research for this work was carried out on Lenape, Ho-Chunk, Eno, Occaneechi, Ojibwa, Dakota Sioux, and Klamath lands.

Additional research for this work was done through my travels to archives, festivals, and in community with artists in Puebla, Mexico (ancestral lands of the Aztec), Helsinki, Finland (Finland is the native land of the Sámi), Paris, France, and London, United Kingdom.

It is important to name lands and people in our work as the arts provide avenues for reckoning and the creative rebuilding of more caring and just societies.

I express my gratitude for many of the people who have made my journey into and through screendance a dynamic experience. You have contributed more than enthusiasm, guidance, encouragement, and the doors to rabbit holes. You have provided the fuel to see this project, and so many others, to the end. To Ruth, I thank you for your invitation back in 2015, giving me my first opportunity to begin writing about screendance in depth. Robin, thank you for all the lively conversations about screendance, for your invitations to join you in the curatorial process, for providing a platform for some of my earlier works, and for your constant encouragement. Thank you, Trish, for your absolute care and thoughtfulness, for your attention and uplift from beginning to end in this and in all of my work. To Doug, thank you for your deep belief in my abilities and for making that phone call in 2015, inviting me to take the reins at the American Dançe Festival. Thank you for your mentorship and for your generosity in sharing your lived experiences, wisdom, and resources. It all means so much. Thank you, Jodee, for supporting me through all of my experiments at ADF with such care. To Simon, thank you for your leadership in the field and for your generosity during my visit to the UK. Thank you for your advocacy, without which the field would be much less connected and much less

Acknowledgments

dynamic. Katrina, thank you for your steady example of how to practice and how to stay curious. Thank you for always showing up to engage, for that lovely conversation over our lovely dinner that time in Scotland, and for your work in the field that is a constant pulse in our community. Thank you, Michelle and Heike, for the chance to meet in Boulder, for all the connections to come out of that meeting, and for the promise of continuing all of our adventures together. Thank you to my collaborators, without whom my creative work would not exist. Brett, thank you for those first movies and for the seminal experiences in their making. They were, and still are, so special. Thank you, Rob, for such beauty and for all the philosophical banter. To my dear husband, Robert, your immense belief, support, and shared zeal for the work are invaluable. My deepest gratitude to you for helping me navigate all of the challenges and triumphs of writing this book, of making my creative work, and for your support—moral and technical—of Movies by Movers. Thank you, Mackenzie, for being a partner in crime during those formative years of my practice. Our work together stands as the foundation for my sustained excitement for screendance and for my success in this realm. Thank you to each and every person who agreed to be interviewed for this work, who provided insight, feedback, and materials for me to view. And to all the filmmakers and festivals who create the field for this work to thrive, thank you! Finally, I send so much gratitude to my family— Dianne, Ron, and my most precious gift, Eben. You inspire me to do more, and do better, every day.

I wish to acknowledge those bright lights who have left our world, and in doing so, left their mark. Simon, David, Marcus, Gemma—may the memory of you and your work in the world continue to inspire.

Table of Contents

Acknowledgments   v

Introduction   1

  1. Falling in Love   3

  2. An Art Worth Celebrating   13

  3. Screendance Before the Screendance Festival   35

  4. The Four Generations of Screendance Festivals   42

  5. Screendance Festival Models   69

  6. Curating: A Historical, Practical and Philosophical
     Exploration   85

  7. Mapping Curatorial Development in Screendance
     Festivals   96

  8. Curatorial Adventures   108

  9. Investigating Representation as Curatorial
     Activism   119

10. Case Studies   155

11. Curatorial Considerations   170

12. A Treatise on Curating   182

Chapter Notes   187

Bibliography   191

Index   195

Introduction

I began writing this book in 2016 with the idea that I was going to provide the field with a survey of the screendance landscape as it is experienced in the 21st century. There would be just one chapter on screendance festivals, and there would be no portion on curation. As it happens with any piece of creative work, the focus of the book inevitably changed, and over the course of about five drafts and as many years, I came to the conclusion that what I really wanted to write was a journey down a rabbit hole beginning with my love for film and for screendance, ending with a call to action. In between these two points is an excursion through the world of the screendance festival. It is a necessary bridge, as the festival has been the platform and the vehicle for my understanding of screendance and where I derive most of my philosophical theory of how screendance functions aesthetically, socially, and politically in the world.

When I began my research in earnest, I realized that little has been written on the screendance festival circuit specifically and that the categorization of trends therein was needed to contextualize the trajectory of screendance as a genre. Leaning into my work on the festival as a subject, I came to find that curation, arguably the most important activity of a screendance festival, is also a marginalized topic within the field. Thus, my experience as a screendance festival founder, director, and curator became the undercurrent of the work and emerges as a primary source of knowledge especially in the second half of this book. What I have essentially written is a curatorial memoir with a great deal of context that serves as a platform and an invitation to the field of film studies to more purposefully acknowledge screendance as an important aspect of the fields of independent and experimental cinema.

Important to the timbre of this work is the joy with which it was undertaken. I loved reliving my experiences as a film enthusiast and how my life, a portion of which is lived in front of a screen, has influenced my curiosities and my pursuit of knowledge. Equally, I found joy in rediscovering the

Introduction

roadmap of my life in dance and how these two art forms of movement and film have come together in my life as a screendance practitioner, curator, educator, and scholar. I enjoyed excavating my own archives to trace the trajectory of my festival, American Dance Festival's Movies by Movers, over the years of its development. I thoroughly enjoyed speaking to all of my colleagues in the field who do their work with such adoration for the genre of screendance. I found exhilaration in visiting various archives, festivals, and people that all contributed to this book, directly and indirectly. Most especially, I enjoyed the bursts of energy that led to furious bouts of typing and the ultimate construction of what you are about to read.

Whether you are coming to this text as a person who identifies as a dancer, dance enthusiast, filmmaker, cinephile, screendance maker, screendance curator, interdisciplinary artist, arts theorist, film, dance, or art historian, budding practitioner, or someone who is curious about the intersections of any or all of these ways of being in the arts, I believe you will find points of connection in this text that will open doors to rabbit-hole journeys of your own. I hope you let yourself fall.

Falling in Love

Some of my earliest memories of expressive movement are ones I experienced through the screen. When I was growing up in the late 1980s and '90s, my mom, my sister, and I would pile onto the couch each Sunday afternoon to watch American Movie Classics and Turner Classic Movies. Through those programs, I was introduced to Anne Miller in *Kiss Me, Kate!* (1953); the Nicholas Brothers in *Stormy Weather* (1943); Vera-Ellen in *White Christmas* (1954); Bill "Bojangles" Robinson and Shirley Temple in *The Little Colonel* (1935); Cyd Charisse and Gene Kelley in *Singin' in the Rain* (1952); Rita Moreno in *West Side Story* (1961); Fred Astaire and Ginger Rogers in *Swing Time* (1936); Ruby Keeler in *42nd Street* (1933); and many, many more. Due to the influence of these celebrations of American music and dance from the Golden Age of Hollywood, I was inspired to pursue dance as a life path. Later in my youth, between the mid–1990s and early 2000s, dance continued to be showcased on screen through television shows, movies, and commercials. One of my favorite weekly dance experiences was watching Jennifer Lopez and the other Fly Girls on the sketch comedy show *In Living Color* bust a move. It wasn't until I got to college, though, that I had an inkling that dance and filmmaking could come together to create wholly experimental, expressive works very unlike the dance on screen I had grown up with. While attending the University of North Carolina School of the Arts to study dance (2001–2005), I was exposed to films and approaches to filmmaking through open screenings in the School of Filmmaking that expanded my understanding of the world of cinema. The opening scene of Federico Fellini's *8½* (1963) was intriguing: silent and stoic onlookers watch as a man struggles his way out of a car filling with smoke in the midst of gridlock. When he emerges from the car, he quite literally flies above the highway and finds himself high above a beach with a rope around his ankle and a man below holding the other end of that rope like a kite, preventing him from flying any higher. He is eventually pulled down to the ocean with one quick tug of the rope and we watch him fall frantically to the water. In these first minutes of the movie, dialogue has taken a back seat to movement, which is used as an effective narrative vehicle to lure the audience into Fellini's surreal world. Akira Kurosawa's *Dreams* (1990) was equally alluring for me with its eight whimsical dreamscapes that use intense imagery, movement, and dialogue to invite the viewer into the realm of the imagination. During that movie, we meet Vincent Van Gogh—played by acclaimed film director Martin Scorsese—and his post–Impressionist paintings brought to life in one scene, and in another scene dolls that have become real people in a peach orchard during a spring celebration. Not all of the scenes are so delightful, however. Audiences are also introduced to a post-nuclear world where men grow horns and are transformed into demons as a result of radiation. These films and others served to demonstrate to me that movies are not just for entertainment; they are a vehicle for the manifestation of our deepest and most vivid human expression.

In 2003, the River Run International Film Festival was moved from Brevard, North Carolina, to Winston-Salem, North Carolina, by the then-dean of the School of Filmmaking at the North Carolina School of the Arts. At that time, the festival was still relatively small, but showcased a robust collection of films from across the region, the United States, and the world in a variety of genres. The River Run International Film Festival is now an Oscar-qualifying film festival and one of the fastest-growing film festivals in the southeastern United States (River Run International Film Festival, n.d.). This was my first introduction to the world of film festivals; I had never considered that a film festival could be a local experience, special and unique from other local festivals due to their particular brand of programming and focus on various niches of filmmaking until my experience with the River Run. Through the festival, and through subsequent screenings of student films in the School of Filmmaking, I became familiar with the concept of short films and the idea that short films are not necessarily a stop on the way to making a feature-length movie, rather that short films and short filmmaking are a philosophy and practice unto themselves. As the film festival returned to Winston-Salem year after year, and my visits to the School of Filmmaking became more and more frequent, I had some of my most profound cinematic experiences in the movie theaters at the School of the Arts. I was becoming a cinephile, though I would not be introduced to that term for some time.

If you've come to this text looking to learn more about the relationship between dance and film, you may have noticed that I have not mentioned any of the innovators of screendance as it is currently understood in my

The Nicholas Brothers perform in *Stormy Weather*, 1943. Film still.

Marcello Mastroianni in Federico Fellini's *8½*, 1963. Film still.

narrative thus far. For example, while I was introduced to Maya Deren in college, my introduction was brief and admittedly, underwhelming. Maya Deren was the subject of a conversation in a class that was more about post-modern dance than screendance specifically and I would not come to appreciate her and her work until later in my life as an emerging maker and scholar of screendance. Part of this delay was due to the omission of screendance from conservatory curricula when I was in school in the early 2000s. The proliferation of singular classes dedicated to screendance in collegiate programs was slow to commence until after the switch from tape-based to file-based video recording formats around 2009. Moreover, the existence of certificate and degree programs in screendance practice has only just begun to gain wider traction, though I imagine such programs may flourish more readily following the COVID-19 pandemic. Another part of my delay in learning more deeply about screendance during my undergraduate experience was the small amount of literature on screendance available prior to the mid–2000s in addition to a very small screendance festival circuit that was not as widely visible as it is today. No matter my delay in learning about screendance specifically, my curiosity had been piqued and upon graduation from the School of the Arts in 2005, I began exploring dance and the screen as creative counterparts in my own emerging arts practice.

My first post-undergraduate impulse in my journey to becoming a screendance maker was to create a multimedia piece for the stage. Not yet ready to create something solely for the screen, I felt that having moving images as part of a live environment that helped the dance expand beyond the boundaries of the stage felt like a good place to begin. *One Woman Show*, a 35-minute solo with multiple on-stage costume changes, five pieces of music, several props, and a constantly changing digital landscape, was premiered in May 2007 after a whole year of work. The piece was my most technically ambitious project to date. It would not have been possible without the technical know-how of my then-boyfriend (now husband!) as I was completely new to digital editing and graphics. For the production, I bought an eight-foot portable projector screen, a projector, a sound system, and a DJ's lighting kit. I wanted to be completely autonomous so that I could "take the piece anywhere." And I did. I packed my Hyundai Elantra and took the piece to small dance festivals up and down the East Coast and to school auditoriums and empty studios wherever I could get space. I self-produced several performances and was offered more opportunities through word-of-mouth. I participated in question-and-answer sessions where I talked about the future of dance and digital technology (what did

6

Chapter 1. Falling in Love

I know?!). Already ideas of portability, accessibility, and aesthetic malleability through digital means had entered my mind, though I would soon find that totally screen-based projects would be a lot *more* portable, accessible, and malleable and offer me heretofore undiscovered opportunities for experimentation in my creative work!

In 2008, I was offered a creative residency and part-time teaching job at The Enrichment Center, an arts and life skills facility for adults with a wide range of disabilities. Through a grant written with my contacts at The Enrichment Center it was understood that in addition to teaching an agreed-upon number of classes each week I would be granted space to conceptualize, rehearse, and create two short dance films—one in collaboration with The Enrichment Center dancers and one with a group of chosen collaborators. Over the course of the summer of 2008, I began to learn about the translation of three-dimensional movement into two-dimensional space. I also began to learn how both the choreographic process and the production process differed from the methods I had previously undertaken for live performance.

Reconnecting with a filmmaking classmate from my days at the University of North Carolina School of the Arts, we made screen tests, storyboards, and shot lists. We rented equipment—a camera, dolly, and a light kit. We rehearsed and rehearsed, both inside our classroom at The Enrichment Center and outside of the classroom, and all too soon we were in production. It was an exciting time! By the fall of 2008, *Folding Over Twice*, my first film, in collaboration with cinematographer/editor Brett Hunter, fellow dancer Mackenzie Hagan (my twin sister) and composer Bruce Kiesling, was complete. In addition, *Breathe In, Breathe Out*, the film created in collaboration with The Enrichment Center dancers and music ensemble (the title *Breathe In, Breathe Out* comes from an original song of the same name performed by the ensemble), was also complete. My first film festival experience representing a film I had worked on was at the Indie Grits Film Festival in Columbia, South Carolina, in 2009.[1] I premiered *Folding Over Twice* in front of an audience curious about the use of dance as a narrative device. In the question-and answer-session, the first question went to me from a patron asking how I conceptualized the piece with no "script." As I fumbled for an answer, I realized then that I needed to start thinking about how to talk about this practice I was growing into.

By the time I entered graduate school at Goddard College in the fall of 2009 to study interdisciplinary arts (dance, digital media, and community engagement), I had heard of the Dance on Camera Festival in New York

7

Screendance from Film to Festival

City and the Dance Camera West festival in Los Angeles, but those festivals felt far away and not like places my work as an emerging screendance maker would be accepted. I attended ADF's Dancing for the Camera Festival directed by Douglas Rosenberg at the American Dance Festival in the summer of 2009, and for the first time I experienced a festival dedicated solely to screendance. I left that screening, which featured works by artists recognizable in the concert dance world from which I had come and many artists whom I had never heard of, with more questions than answers about the curious world of screendance and screendance festivals. During my studies at Goddard College I became more familiar with the history of screendance and continued to make my own screendance pieces. I began to submit my work to festivals that had categories for screendance. My first such screening was at the Foursite Film Festival/ACDA Dance for Camera screening in 2010. To my surprise, I won Best Dance Film for *Two Downtown,* my second piece in collaboration with Brett Hunter and Mackenzie Hagan. My first true screendance festival was the Dance:Film festival in Scotland in 2011, where my 2010 film *Kitchen Table* (also with Brett Hunter and Mackenzie Hagan) was screened. Neither of these two festivals still exist.[2] I should add that I did not travel to either of those festivals as air travel was not as financially

Cara Hagan and Mackenzie Hagan dance in *Two Downtown,* 2009. Photo by Ron Hagan.

8

accessible to me then as it is to me now. Hence, it would be some time before I would attend a screendance festival as a filmmaker.

As a result of my forays into screening my work at these festivals, I began to wonder what went on in the selection process of film festivals and how film festivals worked. As a practicum project as part of my graduate work in 2010, I decided to program and present a screening of dance films, chosen from a state-wide call for films. I received eleven films, and all of them were screened except one. Though the screening was meant to be a one-time endeavor, the lack of films to choose from and the lack of audience at the event—there were about as many people in the audience as there were films on the program—left me feeling like the experience was not a true representation of what I had hoped to achieve. Because I felt the need to experience the programming of films in a deeper way, I continued to produce what would come to be known by the public as Movies by Movers. Movies by Movers was and is an annual, international screendance festival that celebrates the conversation between the moving body and the camera. That same year I offered my services as a graduate intern at the River Run International Film Festival—the very festival that had introduced me to film festivals in the first place—so that I could learn more about how film festivals worked internally as I continued to conceptualize what a second screening would look like. While I would not have called myself a curator in those early days, I slowly became one over the next ten years of producing Movies by Movers, having different iterations of selection panels, attempting solo-curation, studying the field deeply, attending other screendance festivals, becoming a professional educator, and generally becoming entrenched in both the practice and community of screendance.

For the purpose of moving forward with the provocations set forth by this book, I present my own definition of screendance, or dance film (as referred to in some historical discourse and in the titles of various festivals). Recognizing that the interchangeable use of these two, not exhaustive terms in this text signals a fluidity of form and approach to making work that is kinetically-driven, I hold that screendance is one, some, or all of the following:

1. Site-Specific—meaning that we bring viewers into spaces where we may not otherwise be able to because of accessibility, geography, or the actual existence of a space prior to our imagining and creating it. Ideally, work is not simply transposed onto a space, but informed and driven by its inherent elements including but

9

not limited to architecture, energy, history, and socio-cultural matter.

2. Camera-Specific—meaning that the camera is not a mere bystander capturing an event for posterity, rather it is an active participant in an effort to focus the eye of the viewer, accentuate kinetic experience as made possible by directors, choreographers, and performers, and appear as a character unto itself in the work through its contributions made possible by the cinematographer(s).

3. Edit-Specific—meaning that the final choreographic act in a dance film is that of arranging and rearranging mediated material for the purpose of constructing a work impossible to experience outside of the screen. In the realm of filmmaking, we have power over the laws of time and physics! Editing offers us tools with which to extend the capabilities of the body and re-sequence the way life happens.

In sum, I believe that making screendance is magic! And it is this wonderment at the possibilities screendance offers us as practitioners, and the worlds screendance creates for us as viewers and champions of the form, that opens the doorway to the world of the screendance festival.

Screendance festivals, as the only circuit of events dedicated to the preservation, celebration, support, and proliferation of screendance, are an important part of the history and survival of the genre. However, screendance festivals are studied far less than the works that make their way into these festivals. As a festival director, I wonder why this is. Though the screendance festival would not exist without the works therein, the ethos these events create around the pieces they share with their audiences is an inexorable part of our understanding of the form and of our connection to its history. Through the retrospectives, screenings of new works, installations, workshops, panels, and presentations, we get to know this form much more deeply than if we encountered works of screendance on their own. Screendance festivals help to create context for the works that are made in the field. And although the screendance festival is certainly not the only place for screendance to thrive, these events cultivate community and are generative, in that they foster interest, networks, collaborations, institutional and individual support, contribute to the production of knowledge in screendance, and inevitably, inspire the formation of new festivals.

If the work itself is foundational to the existence of the screendance festival, then the act of curating and programming is foundational to its functioning. By deeply thinking about and discussing the screendance festival, I see a profound opportunity to examine the primary activity of these events and how curating sends ripples out into the ether of screendance practice. As a young screendance maker, I would have found a text like this helpful in understanding my place in the lineages of screendance and the importance of my participation in the field at my own place on its timeline. As a young curator, I would have been pushed by this text to more fully consider the opportunities and the ramifications offered to me by becoming a gatekeeper. It would have helped me to consider what gatekeeping looks like and what alternatives exist in a curatorial context.

Therefore, as I embark on the journey of writing this text, I do so with a handful of burning questions that guide my thinking, my research, and the telling of my own stories. I love beginning a journey with questions, especially ones that are **specific, relevant,** and **generative.** These three aspects, to me, constitute a burning question. With regard to screendance, the line of inquiry I'm taking leads me through a series of explorations that are in some instances personal and in others wider-reaching. Energetically, these questions move me, and I hope they move you, the reader, from the outside to the inside, from the objective to the subjective, and ultimately, to a place where you may feel inspired to continue searching for important pieces of screendance's story. My questions are as follows:

- What makes film worth celebrating, and how did we arrive at the inception of the film festival as a place to do that?
- Given the late start of screendance festivals relative to other kinds of film festivals, how were screendance makers getting their work seen prior to the emergence of the screendance festival?
- When and how did the first screendance festivals emerge and how did they influence the proliferation of screendance festivals following their inception?
- How have the aims and characteristics of screendance festivals shifted over time?
- How do different models of screendance festivals support screendance work and its makers in unique ways?
- What is the role of the curator in a screendance festival, and how do their efforts influence the field?
- What does being a curator of screendance require that one know about the field and its makers?
- What is the responsibility of the curator to the health and well-being of the field of screendance?

11

- What other hats do curators wear as advocates for screendance?
- If curating can be thought of as a philosophical endeavor, what might an articulated philosophy look like? How might that philosophy be experienced in practice?

In the chapters that follow, I take up each of these questions in depth and with care. "With care": I believe this is step one of the journey.

CHAPTER 2

An Art Worth Celebrating

As I ponder the intricacies of the current screendance festival circuit, I feel it is important to name the events that led to the existence of that circuit in the first place. As a festival director and curator, I believe it is my business to know the building blocks of the system in which we invest our time, our money, and our art as a way of more conscientiously supporting makers and engaging audiences in the screendance field. It is important to make clear that the cinema festival circuit (of which screendance festivals are a genre-specific collection of events therein) is not a stand-alone entity, but one that is intermingled with the ever-sprawling landscape of media production and consumption. Hence, I want to tell you a story of how film was born and how it became the subject of public celebration. As part of this story, I wish to illuminate the role that dance and dance on screen have played in the development of the filmic arts.

Notice that I wrote "a story," and not "the story." It is impossible for one person to tell the entirety of a story that is only partially their own (as a practitioner, curator, and researcher, I consider myself to exist along the continuum of this history). It is impossible to be able to account for all of the practitioners, pieces, and events that created the conditions for the rise of film in popular consciousness. Those that have historically written the stories of the invention and dissemination of the filmic arts (and of any art) have often come from a privileged vantage point where one's class, gender, and race influence the distribution of thoughts and ideas. What's more, when considering the vulnerability of early nitrate film to the ravages of decay for example, what remains is only part of a whole story as a matter of course. In fact, the vast majority of silent film created between 1912 and 1929 no longer exists. Films created after the invention of more stable media have also been lost to history as the ones we have come to accept as canon have assumed their places in the hierarchy of public thought while others have been forgotten.

Festivals are similar in that those backed by powerful governments or wealthy individuals have been attended by the most recognizable celebrities, have premiered the most popular films, have been the most written about, and have experienced the most longevity. Therefore, as with other parts of this book, I present this information as an attempt to contribute to a collective understanding of the contexts and trajectories of film with screendance as a part of that tapestry.

* * *

The rise of film and the subsequent rise of the film festival was not a linear trajectory, nor was it an endeavor purely driven by enthusiasm for the form. Film and film festivals can attribute their growth to five distinct factors: technology, capitalism, geopolitics, tourism, and of course, art. As we chart the development of film culture, all of these elements, their inexorable connections, and their dependence on each other become clear.

Throughout the 19th century, before the moving image was invented, the kinetic arts were inherently ephemeral. Prior to the 1890s, people packed into theaters to watch vaudevillians practice their slapstick and soft-shoe routines. Ballet dancers of the romantic era dazzled audiences with their ethereal performances enhanced by advances in stagecraft that included the use of dramatic lighting and aerial rigging. As travel writing became popular in Western culture, so did dances from non–Western cultures. Flamenco, belly dance, Afro-Caribbean dance, and Indian classical dance became the subjects of curiosity and wonder in Europe and the United States. The birth of modern dance was underway through the pursuits of dancers eschewing the formality of ballet in favor of a more free expression of the body, influenced in part by non–Western dance practices. African American dance was gaining popularity as the coming of age of jazz was not far on the horizon.

For much of the 19th century, the photographic image served to document singular moments in everyday life and in the performing arts. These records contribute to much of our knowledge about the aesthetic trappings of that era. As photography became more sophisticated in the mid–19th century, artists and enthusiasts alike began to wonder if the boundaries of the form could be challenged and broken.

Englishman, "artist, salesman, [and] adventurer" Eadweard Muybridge initially took up photography as a hobby upon the suggestion of a doctor who said it would help to calm and focus his mind after sustaining a traumatic brain injury as the result of a stagecoach accident in 1860 (Shah 2018). Having made the acquaintance of Stanford University founder Leland Stanford in 1872 while living in the United States, Muybridge embarked on a years-long quest to successfully employ the use of photography to analyze movement. It so happened that Stanford owned a horse-racing stable. He wanted to know everything about how his horses moved because he wanted to utilize innovative training techniques to ensure that his horses would win races. Thus began the quest to prove the theory of "unsupported transit," or the occurrence in mid-gallop where a horse's hooves are all suspended off the ground at the same time. Because it was so difficult to see with the naked eye, and because photographic technology was not yet sophisticated enough to capture fast motion, this theory was hotly contested.

In 1873, Muybridge created mechanical shutters using two pieces of wood and a trip wire, which a passing horse would hit with its hoof. Though he was not initially successful in capturing the precise moment a horse is suspended in the air, the invention of a faster shutter changed the capabilities of photography thereafter.

In 1878, Muybridge captured the first photo burst by setting up twelve cameras in a row, rigged with trip wires. A horse attached to a cart was set to run past the cameras. This event was a media sensation, as news reporters were in attendance at the race track where the photographs were to be taken. Muybridge developed the photos on-site to quell any accusations of fabrication. Much to Stanford's delight, the theory of "unsupported transit" was proven! The sequence of photographs clearly shows the moment when all four hooves are off the ground, simultaneously (Shah 2018).

To show the movement in sequence, Muybridge invented the *zoopraxiscope* in 1879—a device that projected images using a rotating disc, making those images printed on the disc seem like a moving sequence. The discovery of how to make still pictures produce a moving image would spur an eruption of inventions across the United States and Europe, with inventors and entrepreneurs in competition to see who could come up with the best design first.

American entrepreneur and inventor Thomas Edison, already famous for his Edison lightbulb and phonograph, saw the potential of the moving image as a saleable novelty for the public. Edison was long credited with the development of the *kinetograph* in 1891, one of the first motion-picture cameras. It was his paid assistant, William Dickson, however, who took the lead on its design and build. Along with the *kinetoscope*, a single-person viewing box, Edison and his collaborators provided the public with the ability to both capture and view film. Seen as a "peep show" novelty, the box allowed viewers to experience between 20 seconds and a minute of content, one at a time. By 1894, Edison had begun setting up kinetoscope "parlors,"

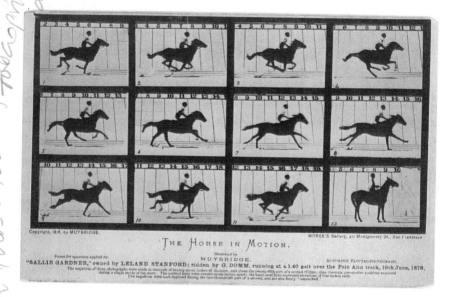

Eadweard Muybridge's galloping horse.

where patrons were charged 25 cents to view five short films, with each film existing in its own kinetoscope. Edison sold the machines themselves for $250 each. With the growing popularity of the parlors, Edison worked to produce a steady stream of new content for his kinetoscopes.

Edison made over three hundred films, most of which were filmed at his Black Maria Studio in West Orange, New Jersey. Among the films that featured everyday activities (called "actuality" films), vaudeville acts, circus acts, dramatic scenes, and cat videos (yes—*The Boxing Cats* was filmed in 1894 and featured two cats in a tiny boxing ring with tiny boxing gloves on their paws, swatting each other) was a slew of dance films. Archival in nature, the films included tap dancers, Native American dancers, Spanish dancers, and modern dancers visible from head to toe, often performing to the camera. Significant not only because they demonstrated dance's affinity for film and projected their intermingling in later eras of filmmaking, but they featured many firsts: the first woman on film (*Carmencita*, 1894); the first Black men on film (*Pickanniny Dance*, 1894); the first Native American dance on film (*Sioux Ghost Dance*, 1894); and the first censorship! The film known as *Fatima's Coochee-Coochee Dance* features Syrian belly dancer Fatima Djemille performing her famous dance routine, "Little Egypt." In 1907, the film was screened as part of the World's Columbian Exposition in Chicago, and Djemille's body was obscured by a series of white lines across

16

the screen. This was one of many instances to come where women's bodies, and more specifically the bodies of women of color, are sexualized, exoticized, and ultimately censored on film.[1] Chicago would become the first U.S. city to pass censorship legislation for the screen. America's burgeoning aesthetic leanings would influence dance on screen for eras to come.

In the 1890s, technological development was swift. Having seen Edison's kinetoscope in Paris in 1894, brothers Auguste and Louis Lumiere were inspired to craft a much more compact device than the kinetoscope called the *cinematographe*. A camera-and-projector-in-one, the name of this machine is where the term *cinema* comes from. In December 1895, the Lumiere brothers held what is recognized as the first public film screening at the Grand Café in Paris. They showed a collection of short films, running about 25 minutes long with musical accompaniment. Audience members were charged a small ticket fee to attend. As buzz about town mounted, subsequent screenings would go down in history as events that stirred crowds into a frenzy. Though it has never been substantiated, the lore goes

Dancer Fatima Djamille in Edison's film, *Fatima's Coochee-Coochee Dance*, 1896. Film still.

The Lumiere brothers' *L'arrivée d'un train en gare de La Ciotat (Arrival of a Train at Ciotat Station)*, 1896. Film still.

that audience members jumped from their seats and "ran out of the hall in terror" (Loiperdinger 2004) as they watched a train barrel toward them in the 50-second film, *L'Arrivée d'un train en gare de La Ciotat* (1896), or *Arrival of a Train at Ciotat Station*. Urban legend aside, this story shows us that not only can the screen show us what moves, but that what is on the screen has the power to move us.

The Lumiere brothers would take their invention and their films across the world, capturing the imagination of new movie-goers, filmmakers, inventers, and entrepreneurs. Their prolific collection of films would include documentaries, news reels, and kinetic entertainments like the famous *Serpentine Dance* (1896). Their only stop-motion film, *Le Squelette Joyeux* (1898), or *The Happy Skeleton,* would show audiences what is possible when one conceives of a moving body meant only to be experienced on a screen. The disjointed skeleton puppet in the film dances a gig, its arms and legs separating from its torso. It falls comically to the ground in a heap of bones. The film ends with the skeleton performing a quirky can-can as it travels out of frame.

Filmmaker-entrepreneurs like Edison and the Lumiere brothers would spark the development of the studio system as players in the field sought to capitalize on the demands of a public eager to see more films. A handful of studios would compete for cultural and economic dominance at the turn of the 19th century. The Edison, Biograph, and Vitagraph studios

18

were all founded in the United States just prior to 1900 and were fierce rivals. France's Pathé studio materialized in 1905 and rose to dominate the industry by producing films and distributing those films throughout the world. By 1906, nearly half of all films screened in American nickelodeons were from Pathé. In an effort to resolve conflicts between them and to compete with Pathé, Edison and Biograph consolidated in 1908 to create the Motion Picture Patents Company (MPPC), also referred to as the Edison Trust. A "patent-pooling and licensing organization," the MPPC held sixteen patents and "an exclusive agreement with the Eastman-Kodak Company which was then the only manufacturer of raw film stock" (Thomas 1971).

Although the MPPC would be dissolved in 1918 amid accusations of artist suppression within its ranks and allegations of copyright infringement (Thomas 1971), the studio system in the United States grew exponentially between 1910 and 1930. Some of the studios that emerged were in direct response to the Edison monopoly on the burgeoning film business. Like Edison, many of the film studio executives of the era came to the table as businesspeople who owned nickelodeons and wished to further capitalize on the increasing popularity of film.

One such studio executive was Carl Laemmle, founder of Universal Pictures, originally based in New York City in 1912. Having begun his career as the owner of a collection of movie theaters in Chicago in 1905 and subsequently as a film distributor with the Laemmle Film Service by 1907, Laemmle founded Universal following the Edison Trust's introduction of licensing fees on film and projection equipment, making it more difficult for nickelodeon owners and film distributors to turn a profit (Schatz 1989). Like other film executives of his day, Laemmle sought opportunities to get out from under the MPPC, taking advantage of favorable weather and available real estate in Hollywood, California. In 1915, Laemmle built an impressive film studio called Universal City. The Universal City campus boasted large sound stages, properties and costume shops, film equipment rooms, a zoo for keeping animals used in films, and amenities for staff and stars like restaurants and boutiques (Schatz 1989).

Universal Pictures developed its own formulas for the purpose of producing films on a prolific scale and achieving international distribution. In the early days, Universal Pictures produced about 250 films a year, including serials, shorts, newsreels, and features (Schatz 1989). The studio received acclaim for films like *The Hunchback of Notre Dame* (1923) and *All Quiet on the Western Front* (1930), which won Best Picture and Best Director (Lewis Milestone) at the 1930 Academy Awards (IMDB, n.d.).

Screendance from Film to Festival

Laemmle's legacy lives on—Universal is still in existence today and is recognized as "the world's fourth oldest major film studio" (Universal Pictures, n.d.).

Not all studios were founded by entrepreneurs. Some were founded by artists who wished to distance themselves from the influence of controlling executives. In 1919, film director D.W. Griffith, famous for his controversial film *Birth of a Nation* (1915), joined forces with world-famous physical comedian Charlie Chaplin, Broadway and film ingénue Mary Pickford, and actor Douglas Fairbanks to create United Artists (Schatz 1989). This studio afforded its artists much more independence and creative input than many of its contemporaries. Actors working with United Artists did not do so under contract and enjoyed full autonomy over their material as independent producers (Balio 2009). In essence, United Artists used the power and backing of its founding stars—who came to that venture moneyed from their popularity in film prior to 1919—to drive material.

In addition to its founding actors who stared in countless films, United Artists helped to launch the careers of popular players like Gloria Swanson and Buster Keaton. Though United Artists experienced financial difficulties in the mid–20th century, the studio rallied and went on to produce some of America's most recognizable films including *West Side Story* (1961), co-directed by Jerome Robbins and Robert Wise. The film features Robbins' memorable choreography and garnered ten Oscars at the 1962 Academy Awards (IMDB, n.d.). The film remains one of the most salient examples of how dance and film can elevate one another when brought together.

Despite their successes and firm standing as major studios, both Universal Pictures and United Artists were considered small in comparison to the "big five": 20th Century–Fox (1913), Paramount Picture Corporation (1914), Metro-Goldwyn-Meyer (1924), Warner Brothers (1924), and RKO Radio Pictures Incorporated (1928) (Balio 2009). As these studios rose to prominence on the global stage, they fought to maintain economic dominance across the world. So important was the flow of revenue from all possible sources that the studio system negotiated trade deals and maintained relationships with Fascist governments even as the United States took a stand against such regimes.

Will Hays, president of the Motion Picture Producers and Distributors Association (MPPDA) and the person for whom the "Hays Code" of censorship in mid–20th-century Hollywood is named, negotiated the "Hays Agreement" with the Mussolini administration in response to a tax imposed on American films by that government. The agreement would help to temporarily alleviate tensions between the United States and Italian

20

film industries by easing the cap on export capital Mussolini had put on American films screened in Italy. The relationship would ultimately be severed completely in 1938 due to "the creation of the Ente Nationale Industria Cinematographica (ENIC), a government-run monopoly that would purchase and distribute foreign films" (Welky 2017). The relationship between the American and Italian film industries would not reemerge until after the conclusion of World War II.

The American studio system was equally entrenched with Nazi Germany prior to World War II. Because of the financial stakes the United States had in the German market, it was assumed that any material created that would offend Nazi sensibilities could endanger profit. Therefore, it was common practice in 1930s Hollywood to scrutinize and edit films so as not to ignite controversy. Hays is implicated here too, along with Joseph Breen, head of the Production Code Administration (PCA) under the umbrella of the MPPDA, in enacting policy that effectively erased Jewish characters from American films and blocked films that could be construed as being anti–Nazi or overtly pro–Jewish from being made at all (Baron and Rosenberg 2017).

Nonetheless, the Hollywood studio system achieved far-reaching influence. It set in motion a boom of movie-musicals that are considered part of what is now referred to as "The Golden Age" of Hollywood film (from the arrival of sound in 1927 until about 1960). These films featured the grace and athleticism of a slew of young performers who influenced prevailing aesthetics of dance on screen as studios actively promoted youth and beauty as an integral part of the cinematic experience. Director-choreographers like Busby Berkeley, Stanley Donen, Gene Kelly, and Michael Kidd and scores of recognized and unrecognized dancers collectively created hundreds of works that continue to offer their audiences the sparkly escapism of the Great Depression and World War II, and the exuberance of a mid–20th-century, post-war world through bodily expression.

Simultaneous with the emergence of the mainstream film industry, an equally vigorous surge of activity was developing that was motivated by ideas rather than money. Artist salons and cinè clubs appeared across Europe in the 1910s and '20s as spaces where artists with experimental leanings could come together and theorize about how to best use their talents within the parameters of the forward-looking medium of film. From these gatherings arose a handful of distinct avant-garde movements, each with their own aims and cultural products.

In February 1909, Italian poet Filippo Tommaso Marinetti published his *Futurist Manifesto* declaring the "beauty of speed" and the "aggressive character" of masterpiece. Inspired by the machines and velocity of industrialization, the Futurists wished to dismantle nostalgia and tradition by moving art from inside institutions out into the world of "omnipresent speed" (Marinetti 1909). Associating nostalgic yearnings and tradition with age and slowness, the Futurist movement was one that honored the transient state of youth.

> The oldest among us are not yet thirty years old: we have therefore at least ten years to accomplish our task. When we are forty let younger and stronger men than we throw us in the waste paper basket like useless manuscripts! [Marinetti 1909].

Militarism and the glorification of violence are notable features of the movement and were part of a nationalistic ideology which Marinetti himself acted upon through his forays into war as a correspondent during the Italo-Turkish war in 1911 and 1912 and as a member of the army in several conflicts through the 1930s and '40s (Berghaus and Erjavec 2019). As the "dominant cultural movement in Italy" between 1909 and the early 1920s, Mussolini took philosophical cues from Marinetti, who was an early entrant into the Fascist Party. Mussolini, inspired by the confrontational

From left to right: Luigi Russolo, Carlo Carrà, Filippo Tommaso Marinetti, Umberto Boccioni, Gino Severini.

tactics employed by the Futurists in their art, viewed Marinetti as "an innovative poet who gave me the sense of oceans and the machine" (Berghaus and Erjavec 2019). Though Marinetti would ultimately leave the Fascist Party due to his disappointment in its increasing institutionalization and widening gap between the Fascists and the proletariat (Berghaus and Erjavec 2019), Futurism left a lasting imprint on the terrain of experimental arts and of the socio-political experience of European citizens.

Paradoxically, the Futurists did not produce a high number of films as would be expected given their interest in technology and movement. In fact, it is arguable that there was only one official Futurist film, *Vita Futurista* (Futurist Life), produced in 1916 by the Ginanni-Corradini brothers, also known as Arnaldo Ginna and Bruno Corra (Berghaus and Strauven 2019). The film *Thaïs*, also produced in 1916 by Futurist photographer Anton Giulio Bragaglia—best known for his practice in *fotodianismo*, or photodynamism—is also often referenced in relation to the movement, though it is arguable whether or not it encompasses Futurist themes (Berghaus and Strauven 2019). Bragaglia established a film studio called Novissima-Film the same year, creating a handful of films that straddled the worlds of art and commerce.

Despite all that didn't happen with regard to filmmaking, the Futurists did contribute to the landscape of ideas and theory through the publication of numerous manifestos between 1909 and 1918 on everything from "The Art of Noises" (Russolo 1913) to "The Destruction of Syntax…" (Marinetti, 1913 in Appolonio, 1973). Salient to this volume is the publication of "The Futurist Cinema" in 1916 by F.T. Marinetti and a handful of other important players including Bruno Corra, Emilio Settimelli, Arnaldo Ginna, Giacomo Balla, and Remo Chiti.

This document references the sensibilities of proto–Futurist experiments with sound, painting, sculpture, light, and photography, while offering new directions for those disciplines in a "polyexpressive symphony."

> The most varied elements will enter into the Futurist film as expressive means: from the slice of life to the streak of color, from the conventional line to words-in-freedom, from chromatic and plastic music to the music of objects. In other words it will be painting, architecture, sculpture, words-in-freedom, music of colors, lines, and forms, a jumble of objects and reality thrown together at random.

Significant to point out here are the references to "the streak of color" and the "music of colors." Prior to their entrance into the Futurist movement, the Ginanni-Corradini brothers embarked on a series of experiments in hopes of creating "a music of colors"—"the mingling of chromatic tones presented to the eye successively, a *motif* of colors, a chromatic theme" (Corra, 1912, cited in Appolonio and Marinetti, 1973). Bruno Corra wrote about these experiments two years after completing them and after the brothers' joining the Futurist movement in a manifesto called "Abstract Cinema—Chromatic Music" (Corra, 1912, cited in Appolonio and Marinetti, 1973).

As part of their experiments, the brothers created a "chromatic piano that projected (by means of light beams) a different color for each tone" (Berghaus and Strauven 2019). With this instrument, the brothers worked to interpret pieces by Mendelssohn and Chopin, in addition to composing their own "color sonatas." The piano experiment was short-lived, as the possibilities for further developments in this vein were limited by available technology of the day. Hence, the brothers turned their attention to filmmaking and produced a collection of six abstract films that featured swirling groups of colors in constant motion, created by painting directly on pieces of film. This practice was also known as "cine-painting" (Berghaus and Strauven, 2019).

Corra describes these experiments in vivid kinetic detail:

> The third [film] is composed of seven colors, the seven colors of the solar spectrum in the form of small cubes arranged initially on a horizontal line at the bottom of the screen against a black background. These move in small jerks, grouping together, crashing against each other, shattering and reforming, diminishing and enlarging, forming columns and lines, interpenetrating, deforming, etc. [Corra, 1912].

Achieving various degrees of success with each piece, the brothers would not further develop the practice of creating their music of colors in subsequent years. Even so, their conception of filmmaking as a kinetic pursuit would contribute to the kinetic drivers expressed in the Futurist cinema that would influence generations of artists to come.

In what could be conceived as a foreshadowing of the emergence of screendance as understood in this text and in the field, the Futurist cinema—in theory—makes use of the body on screen as a site of expanded possibility in "filmed unreal reconstructions of the human body" (Marinetti et al., 1916).

Subsequent experimental art movements would take the medium of cinema to the ideals the Futurists described and beyond.

Dada began in 1916 in Zurich as the *Cabaret Voltaire*, a group of artists "revolted by the butchery of the 1914 World War" (Arp, 1948) who met habitually at the Café de la Terrasse to perform poetry and music, to dance, and to share visual arts and stories. The defining characteristic of this movement is that there was no defining characteristic. Unlike the Futurists, whose work was created to fulfill the aims set forth by their many manifestoes, those who identified themselves as part of Dada wished to do away with formalism in art. According to Hugo Ball, Dadaist ringleader and the first author to pen a Dada manifesto in the summer of 1916, Dada is a word which describes freedom[2]:

> How does one achieve eternal bliss? ... How can one get rid of everything that smacks of journalism, worms, everything nice and right, blinkered, moralistic, europeanized, enervated? By saying dada [Ball, 1916, in Sterling, 2016].

According to poet Tristan Tzara's 1918 Dada Manifesto, "Dada means nothing." Anathema to the prevailing ethos of logic in early 20th-century Europe, Dada produced anti-art by honoring the process and products of spontaneity. Tzara states, "What we need is works that are strong, straight, precise, and forever beyond understanding. Logic is a complication. Logic is always wrong" (1918). In striving for what is essential in pursuit of art, the Dadaists hoped to catalyze a societal awareness that would put an end to the ruins of violence and blind self-interest.

The philosophy of Dada permeated almost every kind of art: those aforementioned in addition to architecture, sculpture, theater, photography, and film. Filmmakers of the Dada movement worked to create "absolute film" that offered the viewer an unfettered experience of time and kinesis as can only be experienced on the screen. Among the filmmakers active in the movement, Hans Richter, a man whose work spans five decades and has contributed much to the field of film theory and practice, comes to mind. Early in his career, Richter, a painter and graphic designer from Berlin, contributed cinematic works including his *Rhythmus* series (1921–1924), which features only squares, rectangles, and lines dancing around the screen. They grow and shrink, travel from side to side and up and down, overlap, and pulse. The flicker of black, white, and grays as the shapes travel across the screen offer the viewer an experience of the dramatic potential of light. These films are compelling, even hypnotic. In essence, Richter worked to create pieces that, through their abstraction, reveal a "universal language" (Turvey, 2003).

Other filmmakers of note include René Clair, a French writer and film director whose work was not completely abstract in the style of Hans Richter, but defied the linear conventions of popular films of the silent era. Clair's *Entr'act* (1924) offers the viewer a smorgasbord of provocative, kinesthetic imagery. We see the legs of a ballet dancer from underneath a pane of glass as she jumps and spins, her skirt creating a mesmerizing kaleidoscope. As the top half of her body is revealed, viewers are introduced to a bearded lady—Clair used his creations to poke fun at bourgeois sensibilities. Using the editing capabilities of the time to great effect, there are scores of men running, skipping, and leaping across the screen in slow motion in a rather absurd funeral procession in one scene, followed by a fast-motion ride on a roller coaster from the point of view of the rider in another. Shadows of images overlaid in a repetitious montage float in and out of focus as part of a car ride where, again, the viewer is the rider. When the film concludes, one feels as if the whole world has been teetering off-kilter and regaining balance on firm ground requires a pause.

Many of the artists of the Dada movement slipped easily into the Surrealism of the 1920s and '30s, which sought to "deepen the foundations of the real, to bring about an even clearer and at the same time ever more passionate consciousness of the world perceived by the senses" (Breton, 1934). Surrealists used their art to explore the subconscious through autonomic processes and the excavation of dreams and liminal space.

Again, Hans Richter's work exemplifies the essence of experimental philosophy and practice through his film *Vormittagsspuk*, or *Ghosts Before Breakfast* (1928). It is important to mention that the sound version of this film was destroyed by the Nazis as "degenerate art" in the lead-up to World War II. As Richter writes in the opening to the silent version of the film that still survives, "It shows that even objects revolt against regimentation."

The film opens and it is immediately apparent that time is once again of chief importance to the filmmaker as a clock's hands move through a stop-motion sequence. Objects throughout the film have a will of their own—a bowtie that unties itself and leaps off of the neck of the wearer, a group of bowler hats dance upon the air, water retreats back into the hose from which it came. Repetition is employed liberally in this film. A man climbs a ladder, down and up and down again. A group of men crawl forwards and backwards, vertically across the screen. The body is an unfixed structure in this film. Heads and hands detach at their joints and rotate in the air before coming to rest in their respective places once more. The body breaks apart and becomes a heap on the ground—perhaps a tip-of-the-hat to the joyful skeleton of the Lumiere brothers. Like a dream that occurs in seemingly unrelated vignettes, this film takes the viewer on a zigzagging journey that answers few questions, but leaves the viewer whirling in the wake of its lingering momentum.

As Richter says in the 2013 documentary on his life and work titled

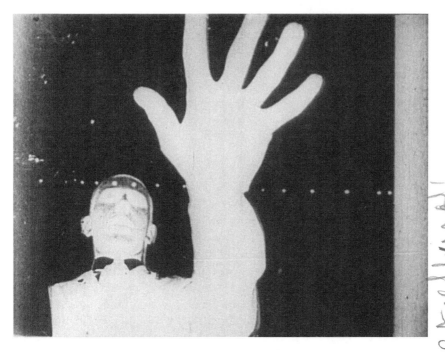

Hans Richter's *Vormittagsspuk (Ghosts Before Breakfast)*, 1928. Film still.

Everything Turns Everything Revolves, "Rhythm, in my opinion, is the essence of filmmaking because it is a conscious articulation of time. And if anything is at the bottom of filmmaking it is the articulation of time, of movement."

A contemporary of Hans Richter, visual artist and filmmaker Man Ray (born Emmanuel Radnitzky in the U.S. and spent his career in Paris) "challenged the assumption that inanimate things cannot have an inner life (Conley 2013)" in his short films that combine swirling, tilting, turning, flipping, appearing and disappearing objects and people, often moving in and out of focus. In his 1926 "cinépoème" *Emak Bakia*, or *Leave Me Alone*, Ray's churning textures of distorted objects and lights up close to the lens oblige the viewer to ask, "What could that be?" Before the viewer can reconcile the myriad possibilities, the images give way to things we can recognize: a blinking eye, a field of daisies, fish swimming under the water, a woman driving a car, a woman dancing the Charleston. Man Ray's films, while inviting us into the transitory world of Surrealism, remind us that no art movement exists in a vacuum. Surrealism was simultaneously influenced by and made commentary on popular culture.

Though women are not as often referenced in the history of cinema as filmmakers in comparison to men, there are many notable female filmmakers who have helped to advance the cinematic arts with their creations from the 1890s and on. The Modernist filmmaking between the 1920s and 1940s gave way to works that challenge the assumption that Maya Deren is the sole female catalyst in the experimental film movement in mid-century America. More salient to this book is that these women challenge Deren's place in popular history as the de facto inventor of modern screendance.

Photographer and filmmaker Stella F. Simon has only more recently been given more recognition for her role in transcontinental experimental film and screendance. Simon studied photography in New York at the Clarence White School of Photography in 1923 and was heavily influenced by the American Straight Photography movement, a style identifiable by crisp, clear, very detailed imagery of real life. She spent the years 1926 through 1929 in Berlin studying film at the Technische Hochschule, where she met Hans Richter. Simon appeared in Hans Richter's *Filmstudie* in 1926, gaining firsthand insight into the avant-garde film community of 1920s Germany. Simon used abstract footage filmed by Richter in her only film, *Hände: Das Leben und die Liebe eines Zärtlichen Geschlechts,* or *Hands: The Life and Loves of the Gentler Sex* (1928), made in collaboration with Miklos Bandy. An obvious mixture of styles and sensibilities from both American and German visual philosophies, the work makes direct reference to American photographer Alfred Stieglitz's portraits of painter Georgia O'Keeffe's hands between 1917 and 1919. It also references the absolute film of the Dada and Surrealist movements of Germany through the swirling and blurred quality of many of the shots and in its resistance to being read narratively (Wild 2005).

Hands is a provocative exploration of the nature of romantic relationships through the use of an ensemble of hands, moving and relating to each other in an expressive dance. Seen in solos, duets, and geometric groupings, "hands are simultaneously the vehicle for an anti-pictorial simplicity and components of kaleidoscopic abstraction and plasticity" in the film (Wild 2005).

Because of the homogeneity of the hands on screen, it is difficult to tell which hands refer to which specific characters in the film and when. Though this detail makes the intended narrative hard to follow, the ambiguity also leaves interpretation of the film open to the audience, which is in alignment with experimental film's resistance to formulaic conventions found in Hollywood cinema. Often referenced as a feminist work of art,

28

Stella Simon's *Hände (Hands)*, 1928. Film still.

Hands desexualizes the characters in the film by leaving out imagery of the whole body while allowing the expressive capabilities of hands with their many joints and shapes to allude to the dynamic experience of human relationship.

Leaning even further into abstraction is animator Mary Ellen Bute. Her works of "visual music" created between the 1930s and 1950s remind us once more that a body need not be present to make a kinetic impact. Beginning her artistic life as a painter, Bute felt painting was "too confined within its frame" (Ivins 2017). Hence, she began creating films informed by cubist and expressionist painters, animator Oskar Fischinger, mathematics, and electronic technology. Her first film, *Rhythm in Light* (1934), was created in collaboration with cinematographer and future husband Ted Namath. The black-and-white film, which features the "Peer Gynt Suite" by composer Edvard Grieg, is "a modern artist's impression of what goes on in the mind when listening to music" (Bute, 1933). At times, swirling lines like soft tendrils gracefully appear and disappear in time with the music as it swells and ebbs. At other times in the film, hard lines and triangles zigzag, congregate, and separate. They appear not to rush. Instead, each image or collection

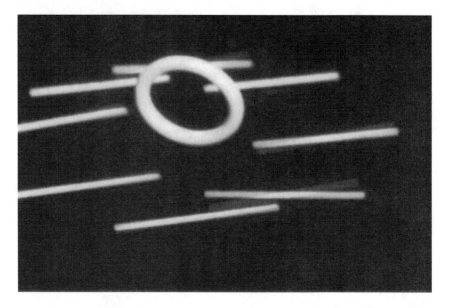

Mary Ellen Bute's *Rhythm in Light*, 1934. Film still.

of images lives their lives, exploring a range of kinetic possibilities before offering the screen space to the next surprise.

Subsequent films would be rendered in color. Bute is recognized as one of the first filmmakers in the United States to use electronically generated images in her animations. In total, Mary Ellen Bute made fourteen abstract works of visual music between 1933 and 1953. Many of those were screened at the Radio City Music Hall in New York City and distributed commercially across the country. Seemingly reminiscent of the early works of Hans Richter and the experiments of the Ginanni-Corradini brothers of the Futurist era, Bute never saw any of the experimental films from the prominent art movements prior to the 1930s until her practice was well underway (Basquin 2020). Bute eventually expanded her practice to include narrative film in addition to her abstract work. In 1966, she directed her most famous feature film, *Passages from James Joyce's Finnegan's Wake*.

As filmmaking permeated mass consciousness at all levels of class and in all areas of patronage, from "entertainment" to "fine art," the need for the practice to be enshrined in the academy arose. It was Vladimir Lenin who declared that cinema was "the most important of the arts" and that film should be brought under governmental control. Following this declaration in 1919, Lenin's administration established the first film school in Moscow called the All-Union State Institute of Cinematography for the purpose of training new filmmakers who could create pieces of national cinema that would challenge the hegemony of Hollywood and advance Bolshevik ideology (Petrie 2014). That school still exists today as the Gerasimov Institute. It is no longer described as a nationalist institution.

In the decades that followed, other European countries would follow suit and open film schools of their own, many under authoritarian governments. The United States established its first program in 1929 at the University of Southern California in conjunction with the Academy of Motion Picture Arts and Sciences, founded in 1927. The Academy of Motion Picture Arts and Sciences is the entity that holds the Oscars. These institutions helped to lay the groundwork for the ideological underpinnings of film studies as we understand them today and had a profound effect on the nationalization of film that is observed in the film industries of the world and on the film festival circuit where blocks of films are often organized according to national identity.

It took nearly four decades of cinema to arrive at the inception of the film festival and the rise of what we now call the "circuit" of film festivals across the world. In the decade leading up to the emergence of the first film festivals, the foundations for the structure, functions, and politics of film festivals were being cultivated via the experimental film communities of Europe. Before the proliferation of regularly occurring film festivals, experimental films screened in the ciné-clubs were accompanied by lectures and filmmaker presentations. Films might also be screened as part of visual art exhibitions or other creative happenings that mixed "technological, economic, social, educational and artistic concerns" (Hagener 2014). These spaces attracted patrons from both local and non-local communities by offering varied experiences that appealed to different people with diverse interests. In this way, ciné-clubs and exhibitions acted as "proto-festivals" throughout the 1920s where the *how* of film festivals could take shape. These early experiments in filmic intellectualism and patronage are an integral part of the development of film festivals in the 1930s and beyond (Hagener 2014).

What is understood as the first true film festival took place in Venice, Italy, in 1932. *La Mostra Cinematograpica di Venezia* was founded as an arm of Benito Mussolini's Fascist regime. Like Lenin, Mussolini saw film as "the most powerful weapon"—a remarkable vehicle for political evangelism (Wong 2011). The festival worked to fulfill a handful of desires of the Italian government as part of a host of initiatives meant to bolster the filmic arts in Italy in the interest of nationalist aims. Some of those initiatives included the inception of the *Cine-GUF-Gioventù Universitaria fascista* (the Fascist

Screendance from Film to Festival

Youth Cinema Club), the publication of various film journals, the construction of the *Cinecittà* (cinema city), a film studio for Italian film productions, and the formation of the *Direzione Generale per la Cinematografia*, an entity whose job it was to control the distribution and screening of foreign films across Italy (Wong 2011). In alignment with the aforementioned initiatives, the glamorous, celebratory atmosphere of the festival emphasized Italian cultural achievements on a global stage, while also bringing an elite, international audience to Venice that increased commerce and visibility of the Italian film market (Wong 2011; De Valck 2007).

In practice however, not everyone felt the festive ambiance as advertised by the Italian government. Early iterations of the festival unabashedly supported Fascist and Nazi cinema through targeted marketing and awards. Some of those awards went beyond simple nepotism. In 1938, dancer-turned-film-director Leni Riefenstahl's *Olympia* won the Mussolini Cup. The film is a documentary on the 1936 Berlin Olympics and is understood as a piece of Nazi propaganda. Riefenstahl actually appears as a dancer in the film in an opening scene meant to introduce the first-ever Olympic torch lighting (Barber 2016). As a documentary film, it was not actually eligible for the Mussolini Cup, which was designated for narrative pieces. On this particular occasion, foreign jury members from the United States, Britain, and France walked out of festival proceedings in protest (Wong 2011).

The second film festival to arise in Europe was Cannes, which was a collaboration between France and the United States. Importantly, Cannes was initiated in direct response to Venice and was actively anti-Fascist. The town of Cannes, located on the French Riviera, was and still is a popular tourist destination, hence having the festival there meant that the high season for tourism could be extended and increase revenue for the town and surrounding locales. Cannes was initially mounted in 1939, one year after Italy placed a ban on American films being distributed in Italy. Unfortunately, after only one screening, the festival was canceled because of the start of World War II—Hitler invaded Poland on September 1, 1939 (Wong 2011).

Cannes would resume its operations in 1946 following the conclusion of World War II. For two decades, Cannes and almost all other international film festivals in existence at the time screened films according to their "political weight" through careful programming by government officials (De Valck 2007). In 1968, Cannes quite suddenly changed direction due to socio-political unrest in France and across Europe. This dramatic shift would help to transform the culture of film festivals world-wide.

32

Chapter 2. An Art Worth Celebrating

In 1968, France existed under the ultra-conservative government of Charles de Gaulle which began in 1959. After a decade of patriarchal policies, many young nationals became restless. In the spring of 1968, a group of student demonstrators at the University of Paris, Nanterre, occupied a handful of administration buildings to protest the Vietnam war and the oppressive conditions on campus and in French society. Their protests quickly gained traction among other student groups and among groups of French workers who ignited a full-on revolt in May 1968 (Beardsley 2018). During the lead-up to that revolt, protests arrived on the doorstep of the Cannes film festival. The festival came to a halt as young people and film professionals called into question the legitimacy of an institution that sought to continue doing business as usual during such unrest. To add fuel to the fire, Cannes was experiencing some upheavals of its own.

Life-long cinema conservator, curator, historian and executive director of the *Cinémathéque Française*, Henri Langlois had been ousted from his position in February 1968 in a political move by some of his colleagues that sent ripples through the French film community. Langlois had been accused of mismanagement of the institution, and though his leadership style was disorganized and unorthodox, no evidence of wrongdoing ever surfaced (Langlois 1995). The *Cinémathéque*, it should be understood, is the very institution Langlois conceptualized and founded three decades earlier from the bathtub of his parents' apartment in Paris where he collected and stored copies of pre–World War II European and American silent films destined for destruction in the dawn of the talkies and in the lead-up to the war (Nelson 2018; Langois 1995). Langlois was regarded by many young and upcoming filmmakers and cinephiles as a kind of godfather of film.

With an overwhelming desire on the part of the international film community to see Langlois reinstated at the *Cinémathéque* and to see film festivals move away from nationalistic endeavors to that of representing and celebrating independent cinema, Langlois was reinstated in April 1968. The brouhaha at Cannes and the *Cinémathéque* ignited a cultural shift in the festival landscape. Festivals quickly became artist-run and pulled away from governmental control.

Film festivals of the late 1960s and '70s were engaged in "critical political projects" (De Valck 2007). Anti-Vietnam, anti-colonial struggles, anti-communism, making visible third-world films and filmmakers, among other initiatives bloomed in an increasingly non-Western, global community of festivals. In the decades that followed, specialty film festivals came into being, creating platforms for underrepresented filmmakers and stories to be celebrated.

Screendance from Film to Festival

As you may now see, it is a winding journey through history to summarize how and why people celebrate film. What is abundantly clear is the entanglement of human ingenuity, money, and power which influences so much of our experience with regard to this art form. As we move forward with this book, you will find that screendance is no different and occupies these spheres of influence in different ways. Sometimes, human ingenuity comes to the fore of our experience as the field continues to cultivate definitions of screendance and imagines places for it to thrive. Sometimes, money and power loom large as we consider issues of access and the industries of independent film, dance, and performance art. Wherever our attention is pulled at any given moment, it remains an important task to continue learning these histories and to keep making connections across eras and modes of practice.

CHAPTER 3

Screendance Before
the Screendance Festival

"Screendance is a history of women's filmmaking."—Kelly Hargraves, Dance Camera West

You may have noticed that in the rapid succession of filmic advances outlined in the last chapter as the first seventy years of the existence of cinema, I did not mention the screendance festival. That is because, chronologically, screendance festivals did not begin in earnest until the early 1970s. Still, this does not mean that the foundations of screendance were not being laid, as you have read, and more importantly, it does not mean that screendance makers were not disseminating their creations through existing avenues and forging new avenues through which to introduce the public to their works.

As you also saw in the last chapter, I mentioned few women. While the very early days of the cinema afforded women and other marginalized groups access to the field because of its newness and decentralized existence, by the 1910s and into the 1920s, the industrialization of the cinematic arts disenfranchised groups without the resources to compete (Wong 2011). It is helpful to remember that even experimental circles were influenced by class and prevailing attitudes about gender of their day. As filmmaker Shirley Clarke says in her interview with Sandra Shevey for WMCA New York about women in film in 1970s, "We've been brought up to believe women are the power behind the throne of a man" (Shevey 2017). As of today, much work has been done and continues to be done to uncover and uplift the "herstories" of those unrecognized women in the field who have impacted filmmaking in important ways.

As part of my desire to support this work and to contribute meaningful discourse to the field, I am dedicating this chapter to two women in screendance whose work was unknown to me before the writing of this book. Their work not only contributes significant theory and historical dimension to the field of screendance, but more importantly demonstrates how they worked to navigate a field dominated by men and to share their art with the world prior to the existence of a screendance festival circuit.

In my view, the work of Pauline Koner and Kitty Doner, pioneers of dance on television, is a significant stop on the journey to the existence of the screendance festival. By utilizing the emergent technologies of broadcast combined with emerging philosophies of how choreography is made for and appears on screen, these women made strides toward defining screendance as a practice worthy of public attention. I encountered their work through Pauline Koner's personal papers housed at the New York Public Library in 2018. Included in the collection of clippings, interviews, and letters is an incomplete manuscript that outlines the women's artistic and technical philosophies. I know of no one among the international screendance community who has accessed these materials, and I am likely one of just a handful of people in the dance field at large to have accessed these resources.

Dance Film Rebels on TV

"The intimacy of television demands real artistry," say Pauline Koner and Kitty Doner, in the magazine *Musical America* (Choreotones, 1946). If Maya Deren is considered the mother of screendance in the United States, Pauline Koner and Kitty Doner are the mothers of dance for television. In 1945, "television" was a word unknown to many. Although television broadcast had been invented early in the 20th century and successfully carried out in small, closed networks prior to World War II, the war itself would stall the impending popularity of television until the mid–1940s and its inevitable hegemony in the realm of entertainment until the 1950s. Koner and Doner would become the first choreographers to use television as a site for screendance practice, paving the way for future experiments to take place.

The women met in the early 1940s and created a series of stage shows at the Roxy Theatre in New York under their joint production company, Choreotones. Each artistic innovators in their own right, Koner was a pioneer of her own modern dance style—an accomplished solo performer and sought-after teacher; Doner was a celebrated vaudeville performer whose ability to oscillate between masculine and feminine characters in her acts garnered her critical acclaim.

Beginning in October 1945, Koner and Doner choreographed and

36

produced eleven 15-minute episodes of dance for television in a monthly series which shared the name of their production company, *Choreotones*. Pauline Koner both choreographed for and appeared in these shows, while Kitty Doner remained a strong support and producer behind the scenes. While dance had already been seen on screens for several decades before the arrival of broadcast television, the challenge of presenting dance on live television forced the collaborators to adapt their choreographic process and aesthetic vision to address issues like the size of televisions in the 1940s (which were quite small, averaging only 13 inches), the small size of television studios, the limitations of having only two cameras, the new technical features of the medium, and the challenge of having only one take to successfully capture the choreography. In a radio interview for WCNI at 91.5 FM in New London, Connecticut, taken during the twenty-eighth annual American Dance Festival in 1962, Koner recalls her experience working in live television:

> All of this was not choreographed for stage. It was choreographed for the television camera.... We had the first superimpositions. We wanted to have a dancer on the palm of our hand. We only had two cameras in the studio with one lens apiece. No zoom. No boom camera, and a studio so small that for depth we had to work into one corner of it.... Everything was done live. There was no such thing as videotape. There wasn't even a kinescope,[1] so we didn't have any record of what we did [Abel 1962].

Despite these challenges, broadcast television provided exciting terrain upon which to forge new choreographic and cinematic possibilities and philosophies. Throughout their tenure on television and well beyond, Koner and Doner worked to articulate their practice for the public to illuminate the ways that making dance for television and the stage were different. Shortly after the pair began airing their ballets, the women began to publish articles and give interviews that clearly outlined their approach. Often including glossaries of terms for a public ignorant of expressions like "pan," "dolly shot," "fade in," "dissolve," and "superimposition," Koner and Doner cited the importance for those trained to choreograph for the stage to develop "camera consciousness," and explained their concept of "cameragraphing," or the "creating of specific camera shots and special effects which become an integral part of the composition as a whole" (Koner and Doner 1947). Cameragraphing was the basis of all of their work, a platform for exploring the spatial particularities of the television screen, and the women could not overstate its importance:

> The television choreographer should cameragraph as well as choreograph.... Suppose you want to develop a movement by giving individual moments of this

movement first to the head, then to the hands, then to the feet, finally combining all three into full action. Since the television screen is comparatively small, a long shot of the entire figure cannot bring out the detail of a single small movement. Therefore you should plan close-up shots…. In this way you highlight the individual moments and create an interesting montage of movement which is part of your Basic Choreographic Conception. Cameragraphy is what differentiates television dance from stage dance [Koner and Doner 1949].

And although cameragraphy is akin to how experimental filmmakers were capturing movement for the screen during that same era, the immediacy of live broadcast and the novelty of live editing is what made the process very different and attractive to the women who saw the potential to reach wide audiences with their art in a short amount of time. While limited in their resources—two cameras, small studio, limited design work, etc.—the women found that they could create interesting imagery and even found some iconic shots for their work by happy accident:

> We learned that with only two cameras it was possible to achieve exciting images: two views of a single dancer, lap dissolves … and what we call a bellows shot. This happened quite by accident. I moved upstage as the cameraman, expecting me to come forward, pulled back; then he moved toward me, but by that time I was also twirling forward. This doubled sense of distance and time created an unexpected, thrilling moment in the dance. Mistakes like this in rehearsal often led to new discoveries. Such special shots created new movement qualities impossible to achieve [on] stage [Koner 1993].

In addition to developing their practice of choreography, Koner and Doner articulated the ways performers should consider their roles differently than on stage. Citing that television provided a more visually intimate experience than the stage, the women emphasized the danger of over-projection in performance—the need for dancers to be both aware of the camera's presence for the purpose of being at the right place at the right time in the dance, and unaware of it so viewers would not feel that the presence of the camera was obvious. In their writings, the women convey how the television dancer must be one who doesn't rely on great technique alone but can move simply with grace and smoothness, as television cameras at the time tended to exaggerate sharp movement in unfavorable ways, citing that such movement "should be used sparingly and for specific purposes."[2] They emphasized the need for dancers to be adaptable during rehearsal and filming to respond to last-minute changes that might make the choreography read better on screen, and the need for dancers to be alert at all times to respond to inevitable technical difficulties in a new and exciting mechanical realm.

Chapter 3. Screendance Before the Screendance Festival

Mental alertness is a prime requisite, for in the complicated medium of television, any emergency may arise, and one should be able to improvise if something has gone wrong with music or technical equipment [Koner and Doner 1949].

And though no such mishaps are documented, it is hard to imagine that the series experienced no technical difficulties at all. Technical difficulties or no, the series was favorably received by the public. So much so, that critics predicted a proliferation of ballets created specifically for television in the style of *Choreotones*. As programming in the mid–1940s was rather limited, the program offered audiences variety among a collection of burgeoning news broadcasts and the first handful of dramatic television shows, sports shows, and game shows. Written reviews praised the work as original and refreshing:

In television the dance fares better than in movies and promises to be a definite part of future programming. If dancers such as the sensitive Pauline Koner continue to de-theatricalize and de-set tele-dance by visually isolating it and aurally infusing it with the soul of sound, it may become enormously popular.—*Tele-screen*, 1946

Designed for popular appeal, the series centers around a type of modern dance that is motivated by a dramatic theme. The programs are presented with narration and recorded music. Miss Koner combines the spirit of modernity with the feeling for true dance. She has tremendous vitality, a fine control of her body, grace, a keen sense of the dramatic, and imaginative expressions.—*Musical America*, May 1946

Koner and Doner held that the dance itself should be the shining star of the production, but that didn't mean that iconic dancers of the day did not help to boost the appeal of the shows. J.C. McCord, Duncan Noble, Bambi Linn, Elmira Jones Bey, and Talley Beatty (who had just the year before appeared in Maya Deren's *A Study of Choreography for the Camera*) danced in the *Choreotones* series. There was also a range of themes and styles of dance; *Young Love on a Park Bench* included three ballet dances set at the London Bridge, Hyde Park, and the Eiffel Tower, respectively. *Summertime*, an original work put to the music of *Porgy and Bess* by George Gershwin, featured modern dance in the "Southern folk idiom" and went on to receive great praise in audience panels. This show was repeated twice in the series because it was so popular. An audience panel report highlights the show's popularity:

The Summertime number was a revelation to me. I didn't expect anything so good. I thought it was excellently done. I had a feeling that movies are on their way out.

39

Choreotones dance program titled *Young Love on a Park Bench* featuring three ballet dances, each against a different background. This one set in front of Central Park features Pauline Koner, as she sings Rodgers and Hammerstein's "It Might As Well Be Spring." Image dated November 2, 1945. CBS/CBS Photo Archives via Getty Images.

Despite their obvious competence and success, the role of women in television in the early days was small, and being taken seriously by industry professionals proved difficult at times. Koner says, "The TV director on our show received the Television Broadcaster's Award of that year (1946) for these shows…. We had to fight with him to get what we wanted" (Abel 1962). It is obvious that run-ins with television directors who had little knowledge of dance and little respect for female artists spurred Koner and Doner's discourse on collaborations between choreographers and television directors. Importance in communication, especially where details of the dance may be missed by a director making choices in production without the choreographer's knowledge, was key. Additionally, the willingness to carefully consider each suggestion concerning camera movement, effects, and editing made by the television director before proceeding on to the next task was necessary to work toward a successful production. The women state, "There is one important point to remember: The choreographer to insure better results must understand the technical aspects of television, so that he can command the respect of television personnel." The expectation in garnering that respect was that the director in turn, would also carefully consider suggestions about how the choreography should be seen by the audience from the choreographer. Even with the spirit of communication and willingness to learn the technical aspects of production, Koner notes that often the women would have to "resort to a person with greater authority to resolve such problems" (Abel, 1962).

The mid- to late 1940s marked an increase of television ownership across the United States and Europe. In 1946, there were fewer than 10,000 televisions in the United States, with many of those located not in homes, but in public places like bars and salons. That number would grow rapidly in the years following, with an estimated six million in 1950, with a much greater number of those in individual homes. As television grew in popularity, patronage at movie theaters and live performances dwindled and it seemed as though the door was open for more dance programming like *Choreotones* to emerge. In 1946, it is noted that several other one-off dance events occurred on television: Katherine Dunham and her company performed the traditional Vodun dances she brought back from Martinique in her anthropological work; Valerie Bettis staged a specially choreographed tele-ballet for Duncan Noble and Virginia Miller; the promise of a series of televised dance lessons with Tony DeMarco (Koner and Doner 1946). However, the commercial leanings of the industry would stifle other shows like it for some time. In fact, it was because of this commercialization that Pauline Koner and Kitty Doner did not continue producing *Choreotones* following the success of the first eleven episodes. Lack of funding for such endeavors, especially in the United States, would affect dance's participation and visibility in television, too. The endeavor would prove to be singular for some time; televised dance, while ongoing, did not reach a more critical mass until the 1980s and 1990s with shows like PBS' *Alive from Off Center* in the United States, and the BBC Channel 4 in the UK producing dance programming and experimental works of filmmaking. Though screendance has enjoyed a few heydays on television, lack of funding and the constantly changing face of television has made it hard for screendance to survive on a consistent basis there.

CHAPTER 4

The Four Generations
of Screendance Festivals

Few avenues for the filmic arts have proven consistent in their avail-ability to and in support of screendance. The screendance festival circuit emerged from a desire to cultivate a formal platform for dance on screen as other platforms fell short of elevating the form to the level of cultural legitimacy enjoyed by other forms of filmmaking in public consciousness. Today, the screendance festival circuit is the only network of events spe-cifically created in support of screendance. Through curated screenings, workshops, networking opportunities, retrospectives, commissions, pan-els and presentations, screendance festivals develop cultural capital among screendance communities and wider arts communities. Cultural capital in turn helps to create a self-perpetuating cycle of creation and dissemination for the genre. As the visibility of screendance works and the festivals that promote those works increases, the need to excavate and identify the his-tories of the festival circuit becomes apparent. At the time of this writing, there exists no complete text dedicated to the contextualization, genealogy, function, and practice of the screendance festival. Hence, I present what follows as an opening to what I hope will be a larger conversation taken up by the field of screendance to highlight the importance of festivals and their activities to the ecosystem of screendance.

Of particular importance to this conversation are the screendance fes-tival founders and directors who have laid the groundwork for the growth of the festival circuit. These individuals and collectives have worked and continue to work, often with limited resources, to create sustainable spaces for screendance, each with their own special story on the contin-uum of screendance history. As with histories already examined in this book, the history I present moving forward is necessarily incomplete. It is explored primarily through the lens of Western culture, with special atten-tion to the United States, and sometimes the whole of North America, parts of South America, and Europe. Since there exists no central archive platform for screendance festivals, nor does there exist a written collection of screendance festival case studies, I consider this work an important building-block in the creation of a more complete picture of screendance platforms and the illustration of a screendance family tree, of which I have provided my version in this chapter.

To fully appreciate the trajectory of screendance in the Western world and the proliferation of screendance festivals, it is necessary to distinguish important shifts in the development, aims, and characteristics of screendance festivals as they have emerged at various times in screendance history. For the purpose of categorizing these shifts, I have identified and given titles to four distinct generations of screendance festivals and their directors. Each generation has given unique and essential contributions to the screendance landscape that provide nuanced approaches to the preservation, education, dissemination, and celebration of screendance.

Beginning with the first screendance festivals to appear in the early 1970s, I call the first generation of screendance festival directors "The Preservationists." Their work came originally from a desire to protect rare pieces of dance on film and create events where audiences could meet these pieces, often for the first time, with contextual discussion and literature. The Preservationists were committed and astute communicators of the value of cinema as a tool for conservancy as well as an effective vehicle for introducing wide audiences to the joys and diversity of the art of dance from all over the globe. These festivals and their directors were engaged in active restoration and categorical archiving. Their festivals regularly featured retrospectives and often included films and discussion about influential choreographers of the 20th century and the pioneers of screendance practice. They endeavored to educate audiences about dance as these festivals boasted a range of categories for films not often seen on the festival circuit today, including instructive media and dance therapy. In addition to their archival work, these festivals welcomed new and experimental works to be screened, expanding their audiences' perceptions about what dance on film might include. The Preservationists initiated the process of public scholarship in the field of screendance and were instrumental in laying the groundwork for more in-depth scholarship and discussion of screendance to take place in subsequent generations.

The second generation of screendance festivals and directors I call "The Delineators." This tight-knit group of festival directors and curators worked closely together to further define the genre of screendance while creating platforms for work that demonstrated their collective values to the public. This generation is known for having a multitude of important gatherings that created spaces where the definition, function and future of screendance could be debated. This generation asked questions like, "Does screendance have to look like dance?"[1] The Delineators took to the academy and produced the first substantial surge of screendance scholarship from within academic walls, providing the field with seminal works that would influence subsequent academic work. This generation is the first to use the platform of the academy to foster long-standing festivals and the first degree-granting programs dedicated specifically to screendance. During the height of art film on public television in the 1980s and 1990s, the Delineators took advantage of the growing popularity of screendance on public broadcast television to share their own works. They effectively educated a public unaccustomed to screendance as defined by this era of makers and presenters. Most importantly, festivals of this era made the jump from tape-based media to file-based media. In this transition, the second generation of screendance festival directors and their festivals embraced new approaches to filmmaking and presentation of those works that would continue to shift as subsequent generations emerged.

I call the third generation of screendance festivals and directors "The Hyper-Localists." This generation started festivals in their own backyards, embracing the do-it-yourself mentality of the digital age while making space for their own works which some felt were not well-represented in first- and second-generation festivals. This era marks a boom in screendance festival platforms following the trickle of the previous two generations. This boom was inspired in part by the connectivity of the internet that made the possibility of mimicking structures of previous festivals possible, without ever having attended a screendance festival in actuality. Festivals in both metropolitan and rural arts communities forge identities, practices, and traditions tied to place, culture, and the values of the small groups of individuals at their helms. This generation perpetuates the growth of what I call "make-fests"—festivals dedicated to the cultivation and screening of brand-new works created in short, intense intervals. This generation embraces the internet more fully than the generation before, experimenting with online festivals and platforms, but not always being able to fully harness the space effectively. The Hyper-Localists shape the screendance festival landscape such that works enjoy a more robust lifespan while traveling the circuit, making multi-city premieres and tours as each festival makes curatorial decisions based on their individual values, instead of the values of the circuit as a whole. This generation pays more attention to issues of representation, even though the landscape as a whole still struggles with representation. Because of the hyper-local, do-it-yourself spirit of the third generation, the assemblage of festival directors themselves begins to shift in terms of demographics. We see a greater diversity in terms of race, age, ability, and gender expression represented on curatorial teams.

I have dubbed the fourth and most recent generation of screendance festival creators and directors "The Collectivists." This generation of festivals and their directors embraces the 21st-century digital experience by championing works made with consumer devices and new technologies, recognizing and utilizing the power of social media to both promote and create an extension of the festival experience in those spaces. The Collectivists embrace the idea of being connected through the internet as a primary meeting and discussion space. Festivals of previous generations are doing this too, but they take cues from the fourth generation as to how to more effectively engage these spaces. The Collectivists redefine notions of competition between festivals, between artists, and in the arts landscape at large, welcoming the cacophonous space of the internet and social media as a place where a free market of self-expression and self-promotion acts as a great equalizer. Ultimately, the Collectivists are about access and putting screendance in places where the wider world that crosses the realms of experimental work, commercial work, and do-it-yourself work can see and participate in it. The fourth generation of screendance directors and curators is challenging the definitions and parameters of screendance as articulated by the Delineators and Hyper-Localists. The boundaries of amateur and professional works become more blurred as consumer devices are more available and aesthetic tastes change due to the constant expansion of media styles and platforms. The fourth generation acknowledges changes in audience attention span, frequency and immediacy of creation by artists, and the realities of the "scrolling experience" where material quickly appears and disappears from view in society. As such, the Collectivists are exploring ways of making and presenting screendance that speak to these realities aesthetically, technically, and culturally. Finally, the Collectivists are actively challenging the festival circuit to become more diverse, not just in its ideas, but in its practice. Festival organizers in this generation are declaring their festivals as sites of curatorial activism and are making decisions based on what they see as the future of screendance.

What follows below is a more in-depth discussion of each generation and their contributions to the field of screendance festivals. By highlighting a handful of festivals and directors from each generation, this discussion makes clear the unique qualities of each generation. Through direct commentary provided by festival directors and their associates and specific examples of initiatives and events gleaned from an assemblage of festival archives, I attempt to indicate threads of connection between the generations. Salient to this work is the Dance Films Association archives kept at the New York Public Library. It is one of the most complete collections of historical artifacts related to a screendance festival in the United States and the source that inspired this discussion. Through the discourse that follows, I am advocating for an awareness of the need for more robust archival initiatives among screendance festivals.

The Screendance Festival Is Born: The First Generation Preservationists, 1969–1983

"The first 100 years are the hardest."[2]—Susan Braun, founder of Dance Films, Inc.

To appreciate the official inception of the screendance festival, it is necessary to discuss specific developments in the decades leading up to the start of the screendance festival. It was 1950 when Susan Braun joined founder Daniel Livingston at the New York Dance Films Society, a commercial organization that collected and screened dance on film. Braun subsequently became the co-director, then the director of the organization before it was terminated in 1956. Known for screening Russian ballets on 16mm film, New York Dance Film Society and the focus of its collections were far from what we would consider to be screendance today. Inspired by her interest in the works of Isadora Duncan, Susan Braun started the Dance Films Association (Dance Films, Inc.) in 1956, becoming its sole director. Braun would use her new platform to collect, archive, and share dance on screen with audiences she hoped to both educate and entertain. This drive to preserve dance on film in an arts landscape that was not actively doing so opened the door to a variety of dance films making their way across Braun's desk, including documentaries, dance technique films (films meant to "demonstrate dance technique on the highest level"; Lobl 1970), experimental films, films dedicated to specific Western genres of dance like jazz, ballet, and modern dance, and films featuring various non–Western dance practices. Braun acquired many of the non–Western films by directly contacting foreign consulates for information on what pieces might be available for screening and distribution in the United States. Chairman of the Board of the Dance Films Association Muriel Lobl (1970) once described the significance of the organization's efforts and contributions to both the worlds of dance and cinema this way:

46

Chapter 4. *The Four Generations of Screendance Festivals*

Throughout the ages, choreographers and teachers have been searching for the perfect method of dance notation, but not until the existence of film has an adequate solution been possible. However, the commercial film world has been largely uninterested in this area, and even in those comparatively rare instances when dance films are made, little effort is spent to protect them and keep them in distribution. To remedy this situation is one of DFA's goals [Lobl 1970].

As the only entity in the United States at that time (and for a time, the world) dedicated to such pursuits specific to dance film, Braun and the Dance Films Association quickly became a model by which subsequent dance film organizations would fashion their initiatives, most notably future screendance festivals. Throughout the rest of her life, Braun would continue to be a champion for dance film, eventually bringing to the United States its first, and the world's longest-running, screendance festival. Among a collection of equally important and elaborate initiatives of the Dance Films Association, the Dance on Camera Festival was founded in 1971 and is still in operation today.

Before delving into the Dance on Camera Festival more deeply, it is important to recognize other early initiatives in screendance festival production. Though these events do not share the longevity of the Dance on Camera Festival, they are significant in that they demonstrate a burgeoning sensibility among parties interested in dance on screen of the importance of creating genre-specific platforms.

Across the Atlantic Ocean, an interest in preserving and screening dance film in the mid–20th century was alive and well. Henri Langlois—the very man whose firing from his own Cinémathèque Français fueled filmmaker protests and the storied disruption of Cannes in 1968—had a fascination with early dance on film and shared Braun's interest in early modern dancer/choreographers like Isadora Duncan. An unwavering champion of independent film, Langlois aspired to produce dance films himself, with the help of colleagues like director Jaques Brunius and art director Hein Heckroth.[3] Langlois' partner in life, Mary Meerson, former dancer-turned-cinephile also shared Langlois' enthusiasm for dance and the screen, and it has been suggested that she was the catalyst for the Cinémathèque programming blocks of dance films and films about dance. Indeed, it has also been argued that she is responsible for the formation of the Cinémathèque de la Danse at the Cinémathèque Français installed in 1982, five years after Henri Langlois' death.[4]

Just two years before the start of the Dance on Camera Festival at the Dance Films Association, and just one year following the legendary interruption of Cannes, Langlois initiated the first-ever dance film festival in

Screendance from Film to Festival

France. In November 1969, the seventh annual International Dance Festival of Paris presented Langlois' *Premiere Festival International du Film de Danse* as part of the festivities, sponsored by the Cinémathèque. And while the screendance festival was not a stand-alone festival and would not be repeated after 1969,[5] the festival and its organizers seemed to be harnessing the excitement of the European avant-garde film movement of the early 1900s, rising curiosities about screendance and the yet-uncharted possibilities for the genre:

> *People are always claiming it is impossible to film dance, yet when Nadar, Edison, and Marey got behind a camera, dance was the first thing they decided to film. Is anything more beautiful than Nadar's depiction of Zambelli against a black background?*
>
> *Is anything funnier than Louis Lumiere's film of dance in 1900? It is all so lifeless. No wonder Diaghilev took Paris by storm.*
>
> *Imagine what it would have meant to us if his genius had survived through the cinema, instead of through photographs and scraps of décor.*
>
> *One searches, nevertheless, and thanks the Dance Festival and Jean Robin's initiative, finds what one has been seeking.*
>
> *From now on, thanks to the cinema of past and present, ballet dancers and choreographers will be brought to us on film. Thanks to the cinema's role in the festival, we shall see works that no-one knew existed, and films by which cinema has tried to illustrate dance, and associate itself with it. Not only that: thanks to this festival, we shall in future see films made for it that will open new perspectives in the collaboration between the seventh art and the dance, something that already existed in the days of the silent film, when the screen was discovering its first stars from the dancing schools.* —Henri Langlois[6]

As momentum for the birth of the screendance festival circuit began to gain steam in the United States, several one-off and short-lived festivals would emerge almost simultaneously. Though New York had established itself as an epicenter for dance film in the mid–20th century, the Bay Area of California was rich with activity.

In Berkeley, the Society for Patakinetics, "an action group as well as a research organization," was "founded for the study of movement to change the world." Guided by the legacy of Glenn E. Plumb, an American lawyer who unsuccessfully proposed a system of public ownership of American railroads to the United States government, the society was formed to act on social and political concerns of the day through their creative pursuits.

On September 30, 1973, the group, led by Millicent Hodson and Pat "VeVe" Clark, staged an interdisciplinary spectacle aptly named "Battery Plumb." Described in a press release as a "survival circus," a "medicine show," a "commercial," a "dance class," a "newsreel," a "textbook," and a "ritual," all-in-one, Battery Plumb was conceived as a two-hour event inspired by the life and work of Amelia Earhart that took place in, on, and around the *Return to Piraeus* sculpture by artist Peter Voulkos in the Berkeley Art Museum Gardens. Examining "movement in relation to the energy crisis" and presenting "alternatives to the waste and rape of natural resources in our country and in the world," the spectacle encouraged audience members not only to watch, but to act:

> What sound rings in the ears of America? STRIKE! ... *The Plumb Plan*, a film by Linda Lichter and Norman Marck presents Glenn Plumb's plan for railroad rehabilitation in his words and the words of his critics. The film goes beyond a newsreel recitation of the events of 1919; it introduces sounds and images of USA, 1973, to challenge the viewer to listen <u>and</u> take part.—Battery Plumb Brochure, 1973

As part of the Battery Plumb spectacle, an international film series titled *Kinesis* presented its first screenings, meant to "analyze the function

Left to right: John O'Keefe, VeVe Clark, Robin Mencken, and Millicent Hodson, dancing on the Peter Voulkos sculpture *Return to Piraeus* (with his encouragement). Photo by Francine Jamison.

of dance in American culture and contrast the medical, ritual, and social functions still vital elsewhere." The series was produced by Hodson and Tom Luddy, who had become the program director for the Pacific Film Archives just one year prior to the Battery Plumb events, in 1972. The film series, which featured a host of documentaries, performance films and experimental films from around the world, was dedicated to screendance pioneer Maya Deren.

This series was truly expansive in its offerings and in its contextualization of the films presented. An extensive brochure includes detailed program notes for each film with promises for even more information to be presented alongside the films during the events. Lasting an entire three months, the film series left little to the imagination as to what the world of dance on film offers, both technically and culturally. Modern and post-modern dance is represented here by the likes of Sokolow, St. Denis, Cunningham, Holm, and Halprin for example, but does not overpower the program because of its robust offering of non–Western dance films. The works of Black dance pioneers Katherine Dunham and Geoffrey Holder, native Hawaiian dancer Iolani Luahine, American-Israeli dancer Margalit Oved, and the Teatro Experimentale de Cali (Columbia) are among the vast collection of films. Films by Maya Deren, Stan Vanderbeek, and Ed Emswiller are included in the experimental offerings of the series.

Reading through the brochure and encountering terms like "studies in religious ecstasy," "analyses of cultural aggression," and "surrealist fantasy," one gleans the sensuousness of the series and how one's world may have been opened through the experience of it. Of particular interest is how the series stays true to the values of the Society for Patakinetics and the Battery Plumb spectacle through the programming of pieces that shed light on socio-cultural issues. For example, a 12-minute film called *Lincoln Center (Puerto Ricans vs. NYC)* explores the ramifications of the Lincoln Square Renewal Project (1958–1969) which brought valuable dance and dance archives to the world through the development of the Lincoln Center campus, but "removed 35,000 Puerto Rican families from Manhattan's upper west side." The film "raises the question of cultural politics and economics, and prompts a reconsideration of priorities in building temples of art." Another notable film in this vein is called *Little White Salmon Indian Settlement*, directed by Harry Dawson, Jr. It's a documentary on the Yakima tribe of Washington state told through music, dance, and pedestrian movement. Most importantly, the film documents the tribe's political struggles over fishing rights and helps to give historical context to other films about indigenous Americans presented in the series.

Chapter 4. The Four Generations of Screendance Festivals

Although this film series did not become a recurring festival, its existence is significant because of its justice-centered framework and the breadth of its offerings. These are unique among screendance festivals that were considered its contemporaries and for festivals of later generations that for most of screendance festival history were largely aesthetically and ethnically homogenous spaces cultivated separate from the socio-political landscape. In this way, the *Kinesis* film series is in alignment with the genre-specific film festivals that emerged in the late 1960s and early 1970s that were primarily concerned with the ways film could address political matters. The inclusion of dance as part of this equation brought an embodied aspect to that work that other genres of film do not address.

In San Francisco, dance artist, educator, historian, and curator Lenwood Sloan initiated the San Francisco Dance Film Festival in 1974. It was a collaborative effort between Lone Mountain College, where Sloan worked as a dance and dance history instructor, and the San Francisco Arts Commission's Neighborhood Arts Program, where Sloan was dance coordinator. This festival is not to be confused with the current San Francisco Dance Film Festival, founded by Greta Schoenberg in 2010.

Running until at least 1978, the festival grew out of desire to "generate an awareness of the history and evolution of the dance for performing artists and to create and extend the dance audience in the Bay Area." Described in the 1976 festival program as a "comprehensive visual exhibition on the dance," film, photography, costumes and other memorabilia were included in each iteration of the celebrations.

As an educational vehicle, this festival boasted plenty of retrospective film material, much of whose primary function was to preserve the choreography of notable 20th-century choreographers. Tributes to Katherine Dunham, the Robert Jeoffrey Ballet, Alvin Ailey, and Alwin Nickolais are included in the 1977 program, for example. And though the festival was heavily geared toward the preservation and dissemination of concert dance, screendance works and screendance history were also held in high regard.

In the 1978 festival, the opening celebration is dedicated to choreographer, dance educator, and dance writer Marian Van Tuyl. Her archival choreographic works are screened alongside her experimental works, *Horror Dream* (1947) with a score by John Cage and *Clinic of Stumble* (1948), both of which were produced for the San Francisco Museum of Art's *Art in Cinema Series* directed by Frank Stauffacher between 1946 and 1954. Also included in this iteration of the festival is an immersive video dance experience called *A Meta-Kinesis Preserve: And We Went Dancing in the Electronic*

Mirror, produced by Bay Area video collective Demystavision. The festival program states:

> This program departs from the traditional relationship between the viewer and the projected image to create a total environment of "motion, light and images." Demystavision presents a multimedia evening exhibiting a "keleidoscope" of live and recorded dances in a unique and ever changing formula. The audience is invited to participate in the "Videola," Don Hallock and Stephen Beck's video and mirror machine which was exhibited in 1973 at the San Francisco Museum of Art.

What is equally notable in comparison to the visual content of the festival was the ability of the organizers to engage important artists and thinkers in the field as guest speakers. Katherine Dunham, a biographer and choreographer in her own right, Ruth Beckford-Smith, San Francisco Dancer's Workshop Director Anna Halprin, San Francisco Ballet Associate Artistic Director Michael Smuin, and then–Artistic Director of the Alvin Ailey Repertory Workshop Sylvia Waters were among a steady stream of guests present at the festival. There is little doubt that these guests added intellectual dimension to the events and garnered cultural capital for the festival as recognizable names in the dance field.

If there could be anything even more significant than that, it is that the San Francisco Dance Film Festival was founded and produced by a Black man. And although this may seem like a minor detail to some, in the scheme of screendance festival history, this is significant because as you will see in the chapters about representation in screendance later in this book, men of color are the least represented people both on and off screen in the field. Sloan is very likely the first Black man to start a screendance festival in the United States and is the only Black American to initiate a screendance festival for some time after that. In fact, as will be reiterated further on in the book, I have found no evidence to refute my own standing as the first Black woman in the United States to start a screendance festival. Therefore, his absence from existing discourse on screendance history is conspicuous, given the important material featured at the festival and the obvious connections Sloan had in the dance and screendance fields.

In tandem with and following the aforementioned Bay Area festivals, evidence for several one-off festivals in Europe can be found. The 1975 Festival for Filmatic Dance, for example, was held in Stockholm, hosted by the Conseil International de la Danse (CIDD). This festival screened 175 films in the categories of ballets and documentaries, and traditional and folk dances.[7] Millicent Hodson and colleague Lynn Garafola mounted the

Chapter 4. The Four Generations of Screendance Festivals

Filming Dance Festival and Symposium in 1981 at The Place in the United Kingdom, a collection of screenings and discussions taking place over one month (Personal Archives of Millicent Hodson). Undoubtedly, there are many more of these festivals to be unearthed through the work of screendance scholars and enthusiasts. Now though, I wish to turn my attention back to the Dance on Camera Festival in New York City.

As the longest-running and among the most influential dance film entities in the world, the Dance Films Association and its founder, Susan Braun, warrant an extended discussion which includes her personal journey to nurture the organization and its effect on the field of screendance festivals which is still felt in the 21st century. Prior to her death in 1995, Susan Braun and the Dance Films Association inspired many of the second- and third-generation screendance festival directors, many of whom are still directing and curating for some of the field's most iconic festivals and making work of their own.

Screendance maker and former Dance Films Association Artistic Director (1994–2012) Dierdre Towers, who came to work with Braun at the Dance Films Association office in 1981, recalls Susan as a "lonely soldier for dance films." In a 2018 interview she goes on to say:

> She funded everything herself. She was very efficient. One of my favorite stories of her is that [the Dance Films Association] was a member organization, but she hated to have foreign members, because that meant you had to put two stamps on the envelope…. If she got 35 entries [for the festival], she was ecstatic. She used to just show everything that came in.

As a small, 501 c3 organization, the Dance Films Association depended on the efforts of Susan Braun in all areas, including administrative, technical (she learned to work as a camera operator, film projectionist, and perform basic film maintenance and restorations), and creative. Housed first in Braun's own home, then moving to a small office on 57th Street and again to a slightly larger office on West 21st Street, her beginnings aren't dissimilar to those of Henri Langlois. He started his film archive collection in the bathtub of his parents' apartment and eventually moved to a dilapidated building that required his own sweat and toil (and that of his few associates at the time) to make suitable for the operation of his organization (Langlois 1995). A theme that seems to run among almost all dance film organizations—even the newest ones—is humble beginnings and steady progress due to the enthusiasm of a dedicated few.

Susan Braun was a mentor to many in the field. She set examples through her daily habits and endeavors with the organization and also provided face-to-face interactions with artists. Towers speaks to the ways Susan Braun and the Dance Films Association influenced the development of second-generation screendance festivals, based on the model and values of the Dance on Camera Festival:

There was the ripple effect.... Kelly Hargraves was working with me at DFA. She was helping in the office after she had finished at NYU. Then, when she went to California, it was Kelly and Lynette Kessler who started Dance Camera West. It was specifically a model starting from what Dance on Camera was. They had the same entry form, they had basically the same mission. Then, similarly, [Cinedans] started in the Netherlands because Hans Beenhakker, who was a Pina Bausch company member, came to New York to do the New York Film Academy program. The next year, he submitted his three-minute short [to Dance on Camera], and he got our gold prize. Then, I think it was the following year, he said, "We don't have anything like this in the Netherlands." That was satisfying.[8]

Many more screendance festivals have been established across the United States and abroad because of direct or indirect influence from the Dance on Camera Festival. Through the Dance on Camera Tour program, the DFA has had and continues to have institutional touring partners that mount their own festivals using pre-packaged selections from the festival. Many of those partnerships have been fostered in collegiate dance programs across the United States which contributes to young artists being exposed to screendance, subsequently entering the field as makers and festival directors and curators. Internationally, these partnerships are more likely to include other screendance festivals, dance academies, museums, and other types of cultural spaces. These partnerships serve to help newer festivals establish themselves by building up their program offerings and serve the field at large by exposing wider audiences to screendance through public spaces.

In addition to the festival itself, the Dance Films Association is a multi-faceted endeavor. Early on, the Dance Films Association began producing and contributing to nascent discussions and scholarship regarding screendance, as well as important preservation projects. For example, in 1960, the DFA was awarded a grant from the Ingram Merrill Foundation to develop archival film footage of ballerina Alicia Markova dancing the Sugar Plum Fairy variation from the Nutcracker during the 1941 Jacob's Pillow Dance Festival. The film was originally shot by Dwight Godwin but was never edited. Work on the project also included scripting the dance in Labanotation.[9] In June 1973, the Dance Films Association held a one-day conference at the Statler Hilton Hotel in Manhattan titled "Dance

Films and Video-Tape, Utilization, Production, and Production Problems" that included screenings and panels. Invited panelists included professors and experts from the dance world including long-time DFA member and Pratt Institute dance program founder and director Pauline Tish. Experts from the realms of production and copyright were also in attendance including Alan L. Rogers (Multimedia Consultant, Library of Congress) and Lewis Flaks (Copyright Department, Library of Congress). Representatives from professional organizations included Delloyd Tibbs from the American Guild of Musical Artists. This is one in a slew of such events that invited experts from across the fields of dance, film, and the arts industries to consider the forms, function, and the future of dance on screen.

For those members and enthusiasts who were not within immediate proximity of the DFA and its panel discussions, the organization regularly published a catalogue of dance films and documentaries, keeping its eye on new productions of note. The first edition published in 1979 listed around 500 films, and by the time the second edition was published, it listed twice as many films. Other notable activities included retrospectives like the 1976 "200 Years of Dance in New York City and Beyond" screenings which included Native American dance contest footage, Mexican-American dances, and films featuring American modern dance pioneers Ruth St. Dennis and Ted Shawn. There were also "Illustrated Talks" with topics like "Isadora Duncan's Influence on European and American Ballet and on Modern Dance" and "A Look at American Musical Theatre."

Publishing the bi-monthly newsletter, "Dance on Camera News,"[10] the DFA took on topics like "Who's the Father of Dance Films?" Icons of early cinema like Georges Meliés, Thomas Edison, and the Lumiere Brothers are discussed. These articles are some of the very first pieces of public scholarship on dance film in the United States. The publication also lists workshops and happenings in the field, such as video-dance workshops by renowned dance filmmaker, Amy Greenfield.

Following the emergence of the Dance on Camera Festival, the development of new festivals was initially slow. Within five decades though, the screendance festival landscape is fast-expanding. Still, the Dance on Camera Festival remains a flagship of that landscape; it is the longest-running screendance festival in the world. The year of 2022 marks its 50th festival season.

It is the work of first-generation screendance festival directors, and most notably the tireless work of Susan Braun and her associates, that paved the way for the second generation of screendance festival directors

to further develop a budding festival landscape that was not only celebratory, but critically engaged with the questions of the what, why, and how of screendance.

All in the Family: The Second Generation Delineators, 1984–2003

> "The festival directors and curators of my generation, we are like a family."—Silvina Szpirling, VideoDanzaBA, Buenos Aires, Argentina[11]

Inspired and encouraged by the first generation of screendance festival directors, second-generation screendance festival directors worked to further define and legitimize the genre through their efforts as multi-talented makers/directors/producers/scholars/educators. Beginning with early second-generation festivals like Nuria Font's Mostra de Videodansa de Barcelona (Spain), initiated in 1984; Kathleen Smith and Marc Glassman's Moving Pictures Festival (Canada), initiated in 1992; Silvina Szperling's VideoDanzaBA (Buenos Aires), initiated in 1995; Douglas Rosenberg's Dancing on Camera Festival at the American Dance Festival, initiated in 1996; Ellen Bromberg's Utah International Screendance Festival, initiated in 1999; and Kelly Hargraves and Lynette Kessler's Dance Camera West, initiated in 2001, the Delineators worked to foster an interconnected network of festivals and thinkers that helped to shape the languages and practices surrounding screendance today. It was because of the slow work of developing common definitions and establishing curatorial practices in the field based on those definitions that the second generation of screendance festivals took a full two decades to run its course.

Most significant among this handful of festivals is how well many of these festival directors knew each other as colleagues and friends who were committed to being in physical space with each other to work out the conundrums of their day and to act as a support system for the circuit as a whole. Because of this, instances of gatherings and guest appearances at each other's festivals exist that yielded written scholarship, laid the groundwork for pedagogical methods through the offering of workshops and the sharing, discussion, and critique of seminal works of screendance that are still seen as foundational to the field today. For example, Douglas Rosenberg began having gatherings and workshops at the American Dance Festival in the 1990s and coordinated the first international symposium on screendance in the United States at the University of Wisconsin, Madison

Left to right: Elliot Caplan, Santiago Bontá, and Silvina Szperling at Festival VideoDanzaBA, 1999. Courtesy Silvina Szperling.

in 2000. He remembers the event as an international gathering of practitioners, educators, enthusiasts and festival curators, many of whom were early in their practice:

> In the room were the people who started [Dance Camera West]. Silvina Szperling was there who started [VideoDanzaBA] in Argentina. Ellen Bromberg was there who started the festival in Utah…. There was the younger generation there, and then there were people like Daniel Nagrin.[12] Doris Chase[13] was there. Amy Greenfield was there. Elliot Kaplan was there.[14] People who were doing it currently and people who were younger and really wanted to do it. I think [the symposium] was really pivotal for the community in that a lot of people left that symposium and went out and started festivals all over the country, really, and all over the world.

Other such gatherings would take place at the University of Utah beginning in 1999, where Ellen Bromberg began the first graduate certificate program in screendance, at VideoDanzaBA in Buenos Aires beginning in 1995, and at UCLA, where Judy Mitoma convened two cohorts of Dance/Media Fellows in 1998 and 1999 (which included educators/festival directors Ellen Bromberg and Mitchell Rose) that ultimately published their comprehensive volume, *Envisioning Dance on Film and Video.*

Along with notable post-modern and ballet choreographers of the era,

Left to right: Silvina Szperling, Ellen Bromberg, and Douglas Rosenberg in Salt Lake City for the 10th Anniversary of the University of Utah's International Screendance Festival in 2009. Courtesy Silvina Szperling.

second-generation screendance makers and festival directors utilized public platforms like PBS, BBC's Channel 4, and other public channels as they made space on their schedules for more independent forms of cinema. In fact, in the 1980s and '90s, it was not uncommon to see screendance on television (albeit in non-prime-time slots). For a time, this phenomenon seemed like a sure avenue for the continued growth in popularity and support for screendance. Ellen Bromberg, whose work appeared on *Alive from Off Center* (KTCA/PBS 1985–1996) in 1988 remembers the show as a "transformational experience" and alludes to the changing landscape of media happening during the Delineator era:

> After the first show was broadcast, there was a big press conference, you know, it was a big deal. I realized … that more people saw something of mine in one night than over my whole life up to that moment. That opened my eyes to the power of television and how important it was for artists to somehow get their hands on the opportunity to be on screen. It forced a certain mentality among artists to feel very much at the mercy of these [television executives] with power. The power dynamics were very troubling and yet that was the world we

were living in at the time. YouTube for better for worse has really changed that paradigm.

Following the establishment of the long-standing festivals of the second generation, and the commitment to creating strong relationships in the name of screendance, the second generation solidified their contributions to the field of screendance by establishing the first institutionally-recognized journal publication dedicated to the study of screendance. *The International Journal of Screendance*, originally edited by Douglas Rosenberg and Claudia Kappenberg, was introduced in 2010. Over a dozen second-generation screendance practitioners and scholars have since edited the journal, along with guest editors from all generations of the screendance community.

Although the third generation of screendance festival directors were beginning to come to the forefront of the screendance scene in the early 2000s, the second generation of screendance festival directors and makers continued and still continue to create time and physical spaces for interactions, such as Katrina McPherson and Simon Fildes' Opensource 2006 and 2007 in Findhorn, Scotland, and Douglas Rosenberg's Screendance Educators Symposium at the American Dance Festival in 2015. A gathering of the second-generation community similar to the Opensource gatherings transpired in 2019 in Findhorn. In sum, while the content of the festivals themselves is significant, the real gift to the field from this generation has been their fierce advocacy for the development of discourse on screendance and the cultivation of a network that still inspires curiosity and debate. Their continued activity remains valuable as new practitioners enter the field and seek to learn about the practical, theoretical, and cultural trappings of screendance.

The Third Generation: The Hyper-Localists, 2003–2016

The number of screendance festivals formed beginning in the early 2000s increased quickly and exponentially.[15] As second-generation festivals begin to disband during the rise of third-generation festivals, new festivals are being created at a rate faster than those dying off (Payri 2018). As a result, there exist over three hundred festivals world-wide today and the circuit continues to grow with new festivals being created every year. This is due in large part to both the developments in technology contributing to our ability to more easily make and screen films, and more importantly, the role the Hyper-Localist generation played in making screendance visible in locations that up until their efforts, had very little exposure to the genre. Large markets and small markets alike now have screendance where there was none before. From 2010 on, it becomes easy to lose track of new festivals as they emerge in places outside of large metropolitan centers. Festivals in rural locations, like the DanceBARN Screendance Festival in Battle Lake, Minnesota, and the Kinetoscope Festival in Missoula, Montana, echo a trend of rural screendance festivals, many of which introduce those in rural communities to screendance for the first time. The Hyper-Localists have been instrumental in helping to create a sprawling, international network of festivals where projects can travel the circuit like never before.

While directors in the first and second generations were personally tied to their festivals, it becomes more apparent in the third-generation festivals that unique identities are being fostered thus creating a more diverse landscape of festivals. Each festival has its own flavor, so to speak, and may attract artists based on the affinity those artists feel with a festival's projected persona. Story matters more than ever in this generation, and the story of a festival's origin or the story of its philosophies and practices paints a picture for audiences and artists of what they may expect at their festivals. The organizers of the Sans Souci Festival of Dance Cinema in Boulder, Colorado, tell its origin story with imagery that gives a felt sense of place and ambiance:

> Sans Souci (meaning "without concern") was conceived one fine spring day in 2003 when Michelle Ellsworth and Brandi Mathis sat on the porch of a 1967 Marlette mobile home in the Sans Souci Trailer Park in Boulder, Colorado, musing about the pleasures of viewing and creating dances for the screen. Quickly, Boulder Museum of Contemporary Art (BMoCA) and the University of Colorado at Boulder Department of Theatre and Dance, as well as artists Ana Baer and Hamel Bloom, added their support to transform mere musing into a festival of dance cinema. What was first imagined as an informal gathering of local dance video artists screening their works on a white wall in a trailer is now an international festival with submissions from all over the world [Sans Souci, 2021].[16]

Reading that story, one can feel the warmth of the sun and the breeze on that spring day. An image of that 1967 mobile home is easily called up and with it, nostalgia for a romanticized past. The familiarity of community is present, as is excitement at the expansiveness of an international gathering of works and of people. This festival feels like an open and

© J. Akiyama ~ KinisisPhotography.com

Sans Souci Festival of Dance Cinema Artistic Co-Director Michelle Bernier greets the audience at the 2018 festival premiere, captured by photographer Jun Akiyama.

welcoming atmosphere where formality takes a back seat to easy human inter-actions.

As part of these storied existences, festival directors in this genera-tion question the homogeny of material found within second-generation festivals[17] and intentionally create room for a more expanded definition of screendance and greater representation among makers, presenters, and their core values. Kat Cole and Eric Garcia of the Tiny Dance Film Festival of San Francisco purport to create a dynamic space for marginalized mak-ers who are interested in pushing boundaries, telling artists and audiences:

> There's still plenty of room for dance filmmakers and producers to stretch into new territory. TDFF prioritizes films that challenge dominant narratives, embody the concept of *dance with the camera,* and embrace brevity. This del-icate, complicated relationship between body and lens—and the creators who traverse both forms—is our focus. We encourage people to submit films if they/ their cast identify as queer, people of color, and/or people with disabilities. Tiny Dance Film Festival promises to be an exciting entree of dance films for the con-noisseur and curious alike [Detour Dance].

This festival feels like a constant renewal of creative energy. One may be energized by the possibility of encountering works that highlight a variety

61

Screendance from Film to Festival

Dancers Heike Salzer and Michelle Nance perform the multimedia work "Wild-er-ness" (directed by Ana Baer and Heike Salzer) at the Sans Souci Festival of Dance Cinema 2017 festival premiere, captured by photographer Jun Akiyama.

of voices and stories. This festival feels like a space for work and makers who are experimenting with new concepts or processes. It feels like there's a high likelihood one will see things they've never seen before when attending this festival.

As part of the cultivation of unique identities and niches apart from one another, directors and festivals in this generation challenge the structure of festivals of the previous generations as a way of making space for more diverse artists to make work and have their work be seen. They begin utilizing digital space as a festival platform and work to create more varied opportunities than those of previous generations for artists to hone their craft as part of their activities. Their initiatives begin to expand the possibilities of what a screendance platform looks like.

For example, Dances Made to Order, founded by Kingsley Irons and Bryan Koch, was a custom online platform where artists from across the world created commissioned works to be viewed by paying audiences. Despite only running between 2011 and 2013, Dances Made to Order offered the screendance community a unique structure of engagement that eliminated geographical limitations between collaborators and placed agency in the hands of both the audience and the artists. Irons saw Dances Made to

Order as a kind of guerrilla space that dance communities were lacking in the digital landscape.

"I wanted to take advantage of the internet and have this kind of cross-collaboration that transcended geography," said Irons in a 2017 interview. "That's how I was thinking about it—I don't need to just work with someone physically living in my city, but I can work with lots of different people everywhere and I can be exposed to lots of different kinds of work."

When the project began, each season was city-specific, highlighting artists working in those cities. Philadelphia, Salt Lake City, Chicago, Austin, Boston, Minneapolis, San Francisco, and New Orleans were among the first production sites for Dances Made to Order. Each edition of the project was guest-curated by local artists, many of whom were featured artists themselves. Following the first year of the project, seasons were not tethered to a particular location, rather, artists from across the world participated, creating an expansive global network.

The structure of Dances Made to Order encouraged interaction and dialogue between artists and audience by offering thematic possibilities for commissions each month on which audience members would vote. The most popular themes were those on which the artists would base their works, and those had to be completed within two weeks of the vote tally. The films (three each month) would be posted to the Dances Made to Order platform and audiences could watch by purchasing a subscription, á la Netflix. Subscription proceeds would go directly back to participating artists, who could use the funds to go toward paying collaborators or creating new work. In this way, Dances Made to Order championed artists and challenged the status quo of financial hardship in the arts. With regard to screendance festivals, Irons lamented the short and costly lives dance films often experience, stating, "[Film festivals] charge you a whole lot to submit, then usually it's one, on-site screening and that's sort of the short life of it. And I thought it was a really unsatisfying way of looking at work."

Following the creation of new works, snippets of the films could be found on Facebook, where audience members could comment and dialogue with curators and artists about the work. Dances Made to Order produced thirty seasons, which included work by both established and emerging artists, some of whom were first-time filmmakers.

In addition to acting as a launching pad for artists to try their hand at creating screendance for the first time or experimenting with new ways of moving, collaborating, or editing, Dances Made to Order created space for artists to investigate new conceptual themes. Some of the films created dealt with issues of social justice. Others explored concepts of gender expression, relationships, and cultural identity. There were also several films made for the project that seemed to come from a spirit of free experimentation, likely influenced by the short time frame for creation and the element of surprise introduced by a voting audience.

Irons and Koch capitalized on the idea of exclusivity modeled by the film and television industries as a way to garner a more dedicated audience. Their initiative attracted a viewership from across the world. So while Dances Made to Order ultimately did not last, the project had a lasting impact on the screendance world. Many of the pieces made are easily found through a search on the internet, and many of the artists who created work for the platform are still making work. More significantly, many of the artists who were new to screendance and participated in the project have continued to create work.

In sum, this initiative and others like it are important aspects to the development of screendance festivals moving forward. As you will see in the fourth generation, use of the internet and social media, the further proliferation of make-fests, a desire to create global networks, and a commitment to increasing accessibility are hallmarks of that generation, inspired by the seeds planted by the Hyper-Localists.

The Fourth Generation: The Collectivists, 2016–??

The fourth generation of screendance festivals and their directors bring screendance into the public sphere unlike any previous generation. Through an expanded use of the internet, a wholehearted embrace of consumer technologies, invitations to artists to create guerrilla-style work, and a commitment to making space and creating visibility for marginalized artists, the Collectivists are changing our relationships as makers, presenters, and audiences to screendance.

As this book is being written, the fourth generation of screendance festival directors and their festivals are on the rise. Take for example, the Mobile Dance Film Festival directed by Andrew Chapman. The festival was established in 2018 and screens dance films created exclusively on mobile devices, now considered commonplace as part of the 21st-century lived experience. Though other festivals have and continue to accept work created on smartphones, the Mobile Dance Film Festival is the first screendance festival to require that all films submitted be made with these devices.

Andrew Chapman talks about the impetus to begin a festival centered around the use of mobile devices in a 2019 interview stating:

Chapter 4. The Four Generations of Screendance Festivals

It was basically out of my desire to create some sort of dance film programming at the 92nd Street Y. I have always had a passion for dance film, and there was no programming for it [at the Y]—so I pitched the idea of creating a festival here. From that original pitch, it developed as a way to set ourselves apart from other dance film festivals. That's why we decided to specifically showcase dance films shot solely on mobile devices.

What is unique about the Mobile Dance Film Festival is that while it is a festival with live screenings like many festivals across the world, it utilizes Instagram as a kind of extension of the festival by posting snippets of all the submissions for followers to see. Even if interested viewers can't get to New York City for the screenings at the 92nd Street Y, the sense of inclusion means that the festival has greater reach than those that use social media only for announcements. Andrew says:

> My main point about dance film from mobile devices is accessibility. I feel like that was the whole point of social media was to connect people, and I'm a true believer in millennial collectivism. I think there's a democratization that happens.... It seems the ownership is in the hands of the art maker again.

And although other festivals in the fourth generation have not necessarily gone the way of the Mobile Dance Film Festival, their social media presence and support of a more expanded concept of screendance making are working to cultivate the most accessible virtual network of platforms to date. Artists are able to find opportunities more easily and festivals can now use this increased visibility to champion aesthetics and concepts not previously accepted widely across the screendance landscape.

The Jump/Cut Dance on Film Festival is also based in New York City and was founded by Annie Woller in 2019. It features many philosophical underpinnings of the Collectivist outlook. With access, community-building, and the support of emerging artists at the center of its activities, the Jump/Cut Dance on Film Festival speaks to the economic realities of many artists working in the field today and challenges the notion that production value is a marker for quality content. Guidelines on the festival's website place a cap on production budgets for films at $300 and state that running time for films must not exceed five minutes from top to credits. These stipulations mean that many will look to consumer devices as the primary mode of production and that the time required to create new pieces of screendance may better suit those who work less-forgiving schedules in sectors outside of the arts to make ends meet. With the steady decline in arts funding across the Western world, screendance festivals like the Jump/Cut Dance on Film Festival and the Mobile Dance Film Festival

Mobile Dance Film Festival 2019. Photo by Marites Carino. Courtesy Andrew Chapman.

are meeting that reality creatively, while acknowledging our shifting relationship to digital space and the attention people in today's society have to spend on arts programming.

Besides seeking to address economic hurdles for screendance artists through their initiatives, the Collectivists are making the screendance festival available to dance artists who identify as marginalized, or who might otherwise consider themselves outside of the screendance paradigm. Gabri Christa, founder of the Moving Body–Moving Image Festival, has created her festival on the premise that marginalized artists deserve the kind of visibility enjoyed by artists who fulfil dominant aesthetics and narratives. Therefore, each iteration of the festival is dedicated to a population that is generally underrepresented in screendance and on the screendance festival circuit. The first iteration of the festival in 2018 featured "The Moving Brown Body" as the main theme. Black and Brown dancers, choreographers, and directors from a variety of backgrounds and cultures can be seen in the lineup, effectively opening the conversation about why these artists are not as well-represented elsewhere, and where their work is being seen, if not within the screendance festival circuit. As a biennial festival, the next iteration of the festival took place in 2020. The theme for that event was "Aging and Othering." The offerings encapsulated here all include performers and creators who are by societal standards, and by extension the standards of the world of professional dance, over the age of someone considered to be in their prime, engaged in a variety of movement styles. By grouping films together thematically in this way, the festival succeeds in showcasing the diversity present in each group it uplifts and presents audiences with an inverted experience of the arts where whiteness, youth, virtuosic abilities, and specific body types are not the norm.

Operating under the notion that dance is a public art and that anyone can participate, the Dare to Dance in Public Festival invites participants to create site-specific work, guerrilla-style. An online festival begun in 2016 by Sarah Elgart in Los Angeles, the festival sees a growing collection of works created specifically to be submitted to the festival each year. With artists creating in the street, in parks, in places of commerce, in nature, in and around pieces of architecture and a host of other locations, this festival makes the process of creating screendance visible to potential audiences and makers. For this festival, ingenuity is held in higher regard than production value thus creating a space for emerging makers and those who wish to experiment with new ways of working without exhausting resources.

As fortune would have it, the COVID-19 pandemic has necessarily shifted the entire screendance experience, from conception to dissemination. As a result, many festivals of earlier generations have had to reimagine their events to encompass Collectivist values and methods. Moving forward, it is hard to tell whether the pandemic has spurred the emergence of a new generation of screendance festivals and screendance festival directors, or whether the pandemic simply highlights the strengths of Collectivist-era festivals as entities uniquely equipped to operate under extraordinary circumstances. As we wait to find out what the long-term outcomes of the pandemic will be, we can be sure at the very least that new festivals will continue to emerge. Some will be inspired by existing festivals, a trend observable through the discourse presented in this chapter. Some will materialize to fulfill yet uncultivated niches in the field of screendance. No matter, they will all find their place on an ever-expanding screendance family tree that offers the field more and more ways to consider, critique, and celebrate.

CHAPTER 5

Screendance Festival Models

From the variety of festivals discussed in the last chapter, it should be clear that festivals come in many shapes and sizes. This is because screendance is an ecosystem that requires varied platforms that fulfill different functions to thrive. Each festival and its unique offerings give dimension to the field and support artists, audiences, and the arts more broadly and in meaningful ways. Thus, I am dedicating this short chapter to defining the five basic screendance festival structures and illuminating their importance to the field. As a way of demonstrating the functions and experience of each kind of festival, I provide examples of existing festivals and their activities for consideration. It is no surprise that most festivals are some amalgamation of these five structures, but most of the time a festival exhibits dominant qualities that signify their overall belonging to one structure or another. The structures discussed in this chapter include cinema festivals, make-fests, multi-purpose festivals, itinerant festivals, and online festivals. It is important to note that these categories are purely logistical. Thematic structures, such as social justice films or children and family films for example, are curatorial in nature. The possibilities with regard to curatorial concerns are endless and run the gamut from a proverbial grab bag of works to the pointed groupings of films like those discussed in the Moving Body–Moving Image Festival. To that end, curatorial concerns are taken up in the chapters that follow this one.

Whether you are an enthusiast, a maker, or a would-be festival director, this chapter should illustrate the possibilities of what the circuit has to offer and what may be possible when creative people dream about constructing platforms for screendance.

Cinema Festivals

The cinema festival is the most common format for screendance festivals. Modeled after the cinema festivals which first emerged in the 1930s,

69

to experiment and learn about the point of view of the camera, time and length, and how it differed from the stage. It was a huge stepping stone in my career.

Today, there exists no program associated with a film institute or film festival comparable to Sundance. Although some smaller, multi-purpose festivals (to be explained next in this chapter) have opportunities for screendance makers to create new work, most of these expect some sort of completion and screening as part of their programs. This was not the case with the Sundance Dance Film Lab, as participants were encouraged to use the time to find out more about the *how* to work with dance and film, instead of producing something for a specific screening.

Though slightly different in their organization and philosophies, all of these fests have a few things in common: they are focused first and foremost on the creation of new works; all utilize short, intense periods of creation to foster innovation; and all projects foster relationships between artists of different disciplines for the purpose of heightening awareness between these groups to create hybrid material. For makers for whom collegiate programs are out of reach, or who have come to the practice post-education, or from another experience completely, these programs offer a space to gain the tools needed to make pieces that are both artful and display technical know-how. Most importantly, these types of festivals provide training grounds and environments for supported experimentation for new screendance makers, many utilizing these platforms to make their very first films. For the screendance festival landscape at large, make-fests provide a place to maintain a flow of makers and their works steadily feeding the circuit.

Multi-Purpose Festivals

Is a screendance festival a stand-alone entity? Or can the concept of "festival" be expanded to include those that happen in conjunction with other events? We see from some of the first iterations of screendance festivals in the 20th century that multi-purpose festivals have historically helped screendance and its presence in the public art scene to thrive. In both the Festival International du Film de Danse initiated by Henri Langlois and the Kinesis screenings as part of the Battery Plum Review produced by Millicent Hodson, these events were presented as part of larger celebrations of art. Today, many screendance directors and curators find that partnerships and multi-faceted events help their resources go farther and make visible the correlations screendance shares with other art forms.

Multi-purpose festivals are ones which incorporate screendance showings among other types of work such as live dance and theatrical performance, live music, visual art, craft, and other types of films. By placing screendance among a constellation of various art forms, multi-purpose festivals have the potential to achieve a level of visibility for screendance that other models may not. As patrons to these events get swept up in the flow of all there is to see and do, they may be more open to viewing something they may know very little about because of the inherent variance and novelty of the multi-purpose festival experience.

The Cucalorus Festival in Wilmington, North Carolina,[4] for example, includes several branches: film, which includes stand-alone screendance blocks in addition to screendance works programmed as part of short-film blocks curated along thematic lines; live performance including dance, music, and theater; a technology conference called "Connect"; and an evolving roster of special events that varies each season. A festival like Cucalorus helps to bridge the gap between cinema and screendance by normalizing it within a selection of films of all types. As a mid-size festival that is both grant- and privately supported, Cucalorus has the capacity to focus on creating the conditions for networking among artists in active ways where screendance festivals smaller in scope may not have the resources to do so. Brigid Greene, a curator from the Cucalorus Festival, stresses that "the Cucalorous is really for the artists." She notes how the festival is able to support artists through housing and stipends for their work, which opens more possibilities for collaborative relationships to bloom. Each year, Greene says, "The web expands. All the little invisible links are made a little bit more apparent."

Much of the success of a festival like Cucalorus hinges on creative and effective community engagement, something that many screendance festivals struggle with due to a lack of financial resources and manpower. The festival uses its community initiatives to promote a horizontal organizational atmosphere where community members can feel personally invested in the festival, therefore more apt to support the festival's events through attendance, peer-to-peer promotion, and tax-deductible donations.

> Every Tuesday, there's a "Main Brain," which, if you're based in North Carolina, is an open brainstorming session. It's a staff meeting, but for anyone who wants to come. Sometimes it's more work-heavy than other times. Sometimes it's more fun. Sometimes some of the films that have been submitted are watched in Main Brain. It's used for many different things, but it's certainly to serve as a sort of model of ways in which a non-hierarchical organizational structure can exist.

This unique combination of multilayered celebration, reliable and practical support for artists and their work, and inclusive community engagement make the Cucalorus Festival a popular destination for screendance makers across the United States.

Through a collaborative partnership with the Grounds for Sculpture[5] in Hamilton, New Jersey, The Outlet Dance Project produces an annual series of dance, visual art, and screendance events for the public. Founded in 2005 by dance artist Jamuna Chiarini, The Outlet Dance Project began by featuring only live performance among the sculptures on display at the Grounds, as well as among the rotating exhibitions in the indoor galleries. In 2011, the festival expanded to include screendance offerings, co-curated by Associate Director Ann Robideaux and Executive Director Donia Salem Harhoor. With a focus on women and female-identified choreographers, dancers, and filmmakers, the festival invites audiences to consider the experience of the arts in multi-dimensional ways that help audiences make connections between site, the body, objects, and the conceptual and aesthetic possibilities of all of those on screen through the equal billing of each component. Salem Harhoor says:

> One thing that is notable is because the day of dance is at the Grounds for Sculpture, we naturally want to see and explore intersections between traditional visual arts and moving arts [in dance film]. We want to see how place influences dance film, how locations and movement interact and interweave in different ways. And also—not that we exclusively take only site-specific films—but we take films that are in relationship to sculpture, to exploring the visual art aspect of dance in different ways.

Each year The Outlet Dance Project attracts artists from across the world to participate in both the live and digital portions of the festival. Their participation brings a multi-dimensional aspect to the festival that both aligns with and extends beyond the interdisciplinary character of the festival as it is structured.

The function of multi-purpose festivals among the constellation of festival formats does the work of integrating screendance into the broader landscape of the arts and introduces audiences already willing to engage with other types of arts to screendance. In addition, multi-purpose festivals provide stimulative platforms for both artists and audiences to have three-dimensional artistic experiences that bolster support for the arts as a whole. As support for the arts in the West continues to decline, the partnerships inherent within multi-purpose festivals with organizations and communities means that these festivals have access to resources often not available to more traditional festivals, whether it be in-kind space, the ability to increase fundraising power, or to garner broad volunteer support from the communities these festivals serve. Multi-purpose festivals high-light the dynamism of the arts and demonstrate the ways that screendance continues to contribute to the arts ecosystem in valuable ways.

Itinerant Festivals

One of the ways festivals can extend their reach in live space is to cre-ate opportunities for their selections to travel to meet audiences where they are, instead of expecting audiences to come to one location to see the work. Itinerant festivals expand the influence of screendance works by cre-ating opportunities to have multiple conversations about the work in var-ious contexts that may serve to reveal nuances in the works that only one screening, with one audience, may not reveal. While many festivals have adopted the practice of touring rosters of works through partnerships with universities and community organizations as a way of enlarging the scope of their events, few are structured as truly itinerant festivals with a commit-ment to touring as the primary function and character of the festival.

One of the most notable itinerant festivals is the Agite y Sirve Festival in Mexico, founded by Ximena Monroy. For locations where artists wish to develop a more robust screendance awareness and community, Monroy insists that itinerant festivals are effective in fulfilling that desire:

> The Agite y Sirve Festival was founded in 2008, having its first edition in 2009. Each year it takes place in Mexico City, Oaxaca and Puebla. I imagined an itin-erant festival from knowing the work involved in an edition that happens once a year in one city. With the aim of promoting and strengthening screendance in Mexico, I thought of using the management of an edition to cover more than one city. While we carry out full editions in three cities, we have activities almost throughout the year, thanks to the itinerant nature of the festival. Most of the festival's itineraries work through invitations from institutions or other festivals, and thanks to the co-production between them and Agite y Sirva. For example, we are part of the National Dance Festivals Network from INBA [Instituto Nacional de Bellas Artes (National Institute of Fine Arts)].

Since its inception, the Agite y Sirve Festival has traveled to more than 60 cities in Mexico, Latin America, North America and Europe. The festival also publishes literature on screendance and helps engage artists through regular workshops and panels.

Because of the necessity of truly itinerant festivals to have many sta-ble partnerships to be sustainable, the work involved with creating and maintaining these festivals makes them rare. Even so, itinerant festivals are important aspects of the screendance festival ecosystem as they put screendance in front of wider audiences.

Online Festivals

As our lives become more and more intertwined with digital space, it is no wonder that screendance turns to the internet as festival space. It is relatively accessible, affordable, and puts work in front of far more people than a single, live film-festival event can. While early online festivals including the UMove Online Videodance Festival (founded in 2009, arguably the first online screendance festival) and Dances Made to Order, a subscription-based initiative (founded in 2011), have not stood the test of time, other festivals have emerged to fill their void.

Sarah Elgart's Dare to Dance in Public Film Festival, founded in 2016, aims to democratize dance and challenge artists and audiences to consider when and where dance belongs in the world. Produced through the Los Angeles–based online publication, *Cultural Weekly*, and supported year-round through Elgart's own blog on that publication titled *Screendance Diaries*, the festival invites artists who are interested in "democratizing dance, challenging notions of a proper time & place for it to happen, and sharing it on film" to participate (D2D, 2021). A 2019 call for films continues, "Polished or raw, we invite you to make or find a dance in a public place, shoot it, share it, and enter it. Get your work seen by … thousands of online readers. Burst out of the studio or theater and onto streets, subways, supermarket aisles and beyond…. Dance it, shoot it, and share it…. We dare you to!"

The invitation here encourages not only engagement by viewers online, but gets the process of filmmaking out into public spaces where people may be introduced to screendance through seeing performers move through public spaces in front of, or being followed by cameras. Although the festival is ultimately deployed online, we see in this instance that the live components of screendance remain as important as the product and that visibility of all aspects of screendance may help increase support for and interest in the genre by non-dance filmmakers.

As more online festivals emerge on the screendance festival circuit, varied models of dissemination emerge, too. The FilmFest by Rogue Dancer, also known as Jennifer Scully-Thurston, is a monthly, online screendance festival founded in 2019 that publishes theme-specific screenings for a limited amount of time for patrons to enjoy. Some of the themes for the 2020 season include "BODY Landscape," "Travel," and "Fantasy." Some of the monthly online screenings are augmented with live screenings that may also have live dance as well. Like Dare to Dance in Public, the festival is deployed through a website (Scully-Thurston's self-designed site) where blog posts are published on a number of subjects related to dance and dance film. In a 2019 interview, Scully-Thurston comprehensively explains the impetus behind the festival and her opinions about how it functions in service to both dance and screendance:

> As an aging dancer, I'm trying to carve out a space for myself in the dance world. My goal is to serve the dance community, and it's important to me that the dance work gets seen. So this is my way of bridging the gap between live performance and people not having access to see the work. And that includes a film festival, I think. And so I want to create an opportunity where [dance] can be shareable, people can sit in their own homes, have kind of a Netflix experience for dance film festivals. But the purpose is to also open the eyes of the general public to see what's out there. I've always said that I don't think it's that people don't like dance, I think people just don't know dance. So, unless you have kind of an incestuous audience where it's dancers watching dance, which is often how it is, this is my way to lift the veil on choreographers and filmmakers. I mean, it's almost surprising how many choreographers are making films. They're making films that are a real marriage of filmmaking and choreography. There's dancing cameras, there's dancing people, they're doing it all over the world, they're doing it in many different places, they're animating…. It's a really rich culture of dance work. And when you curate a festival at a brick-and-mortar event, you have limitations of space, there's a time limitation and there's an audience limitation. There's a certain amount of hours you can put in front of people live, and it's really hard to have hundreds of hours of film and to have to say no to most of the filmmakers that submit. So, to me, that's a heartbreaking situation for myself as a curator, a dancer, and a choreographer. So this online festival is another way to say yes to the artist, to give artists the feeling that they are making relevant work in today's culture.

As one can glean from the examples of Elgart and Scully-Thurston's festivals, one of the main functions of online screendance festivals is to capitalize on the visibility that the internet provides while situating screendance as a part of mainstream society. With the ever-present reality of screens and our interactions with them more and more prevalent, the creation of more online screendance festivals is imminent. In the midst of the COVID-19 pandemic of 2020, almost all festivals became online festivals as a matter of course, challenging the screendance community at large to reconsider the ways festivals are produced, who they serve, and how.

Online festivals are effectively changing our understanding of what screendance is and who makes it. In online spaces that constantly turn over new content, the pressure to create something that is of high production value—which is a blurry concept these days as the capabilities of consumer technology continues to improve—diminishes. Online makers, their works, and online festivals showcase the ways low-stakes experimentation over time may help filmmakers learn new skills, develop new ideas, and share those discoveries with audiences. Online, the expectations of those audiences may be different than those held when entering live performance spaces or more traditional film venues. Furthermore, online festivals allow their organizers to be more generous with the content they choose, often programming more films than if there were restrictions on space and time, one of the challenges of programming for live festivals.

Summing Up the Festival Landscape

Since the emergence of the screendance festival and its journey into the 21st century, some through lines appear that can help us to consider the significance and the utility of such festivals. As an ephemeral art, the first impulse of the screendance community was to use the permanence of film to archive notable works of dance. As we continue deeper into our relationship and existence alongside screens, it would seem that most live art now *must* be considered through the context of screens in some way, whether for the purpose of documentation, promotion, or whether the medium itself is of main interest. Like their forerunners, contemporary screendance festivals are about encapsulating both the canonical and the new, while placing on display the aesthetic concerns of the time they exist in. Screendance festivals, whether focused on preservation or bold experimentation, are about acting as time capsules. In keeping with the development of cinema itself, dance has been a natural commendation to the cinematic arts since its invention and has opened the door to experimental ways of working that created what we now know to be screendance. As screendance makers in the early and mid–20th century worked to find spaces for their work to be accepted and seen by audiences, many turned to the platforms available at the time—existing cinema festivals, television, and experimental art spaces. Although these spaces worked for a handful of artists, the growing majority of screendance makers lacked a platform that would champion their work and provide needed community networks. As screendance festivals trickled into existence between the 1970s and early 2000s, a close-knit kinship was formed that offered the world opportunities for the celebration of screendance works, critical dialogue about screendance, and a base from which to build audiences to support the growth and survival of screendance. Older screendance festivals influenced and continue to influence the development of newer screendance festivals and the genealogy of the first generations of screendance festivals and directors is evident and worthy of recognition as vital parts of our history. Since the global screendance festival boom after 2010, the sprawling network of festivals now offers screendance makers a multitude of ways to share their work from in-person screenings to collaborative learning environments to online platforms.

In the spring of 2018, screendance scholar Blas Payri's article "Life and Death of Screendance Festivals: a Panorama" was published in the *Journal of Videodance Studies*, a publication out of Valencia, Spain.[6] It persists as one of the few publications available in the screendance community that addresses the state of screendance festivals with regard to their lifecycles. In that article, Payri notes that there are 267 active festivals findable online for the year 2018. And while this information is now outdated—the screendance festival landscape continues to shift each year—it remains true for the time being at least, that new festivals are being born at a rate faster than older festivals are dying. What also remains true are the challenges to maintaining screendance festivals which can be attributed to the realities of funding, spatial resources, and the generally small, mostly-volunteer teams that run screendance festivals. In fact, so many festivals are so closely tied to the personal lives of many of their founders, directors, and curators that operations may be suspended or modified for a number of reasons— giving birth (which speaks to the gendered landscape of festival directors and curators in the West), socio-political events, job changes, and more. Even with the opportunity for screendance works to "travel the circuit" of screendance festivals exclusively and screendance makers to meet audiences and other makers around the world, the circuit still lacks a critical mass of festivals with the power to provide wide distribution, opportunities for substantial financial gains, and opportunities to meet the industry in ways that yield many professional opportunities outside of the screendance and dance realms. As Mark Peranson explains in his scholarship on cinema festivals, there exist two kinds of cinema festivals: industry festivals and audience festivals. Industry festivals are those that boast the presence of industry professionals and create space for market activity. Only the very largest cinema festivals can do this on a regular basis and, as discussed earlier in previous chapters, some screendance works have been successful in being included in those festivals. Audience festivals are often artist-driven and more about enthusiasm for the work rather than selling work. Screendance festivals almost always fall into this category given the small organizational teams and volunteer culture inherent in screendance festivals. Additionally, screendance festivals often cater to those already interested in screendance. Whether or not this is intentional may speak to a larger conundrum facing the screendance community that concerns the challenges of building and sustaining new audiences. Anecdotally, it would seem that while many admit to the struggle of not having an economy, there is a general disdain for a monied market among screendance communities.

Even though the screendance festival landscape has not yet been wildly successful in extending its reach beyond its own network, there are many good outcomes to a broadening landscape. In addition to works being able to truly "travel the circuit" of screendance festivals in recent history, other benefits include more scholarship, teaching, and ongoing conversations about the future of screendance and screendance festivals. Most of all, screendance festivals provide spaces where those interested in the field can get the most comprehensive education. Although there have emerged a handful of collegiate programs dedicated to the study and practice of screendance, the experience of the screendance festival offers interactions with wide selections of work, the possibility of face-to-face exchanges with artists, festival directors, and curators, and a host of activities related to dialogue, workshopping new material, critical analysis, hands-on collaboration, and more. As has been the trend from the beginning of the screendance festival landscape, the community created as a result of the practice of screendance remains its most valuable resource. The events, products, and relationships generated as a result of an active festival landscape continue to ensure the survival of screendance.

CHAPTER 6

Curating:
A Historical, Practical
and Philosophical Exploration

Thoughts on Becoming a Curator

Having explored the development, the forms, and the functions of the screendance festival from an objective view, I turn now to the topic of the felt experience of a festival, informed most saliently by the works included in any specific event. As one of the primary activities of a screendance festival team is to select and screen works, it is necessary to explore the act of curating from both a philosophical perspective and an embodied one. What does it mean to curate?

Curating is a subjective endeavor. Many of the field's most recognized actors articulate for us their respective philosophies influenced by the ethos of their particular eras, their experiences with regard to exposure to art, their trajectory of education and training in curating, be it formal or informal, and their intrinsic morals and values. Often, this means that philosophies on curating and ways of practicing, while overlapping, do not align to create one, neat definition of what the practice entails. For example, the Artistic Director of Serpentine Galleries in London, Hans Ulrich Obrist says:

> I don't believe in the creativity of the curator. I don't think that the
> exhibition-maker has brilliant ideas around which the works of artists must fit.
> Instead, the process always starts with a conversation, in which I ask the artists
> what their unrealized projects are, and then the task is to find the means to real-
> ize them [Kuoni 2001].

Conversely, Mari Carmen Rodriquez, Wortham Curator of Latin American Art at the Museum of Fine Arts, Houston, says:

> I believe that curatorial practice entails a creative and imaginative dimension
> that is somewhat parallel to that of the artist and even closer to that of the critic.

Screendance from Film to Festival

This is not to say that the curator should take the artist's place, as some detractors have naïvely suggested. Rather, it implies acknowledging that curatorship involves a propositional discourse that invariably results in some form of "scenic enunciation," whether by means of an exhibition or other concrete manifestation of the curatorial proposal [Kuoni 2001].

In screendance, we also have our philosophers; those who articulate in tidy sound bites the experience of curating and presenting dance films. Kelly Hargraves of Dance Camera West says:

> I think of dance films like music, like little pop songs. I like shorts. [When curating] I'm creating an album, a mix-tape that people can pay attention to and enjoy not only visually…. I'm also about the energy of performance coming through the camera. I have to put it all together to tell a story, one way or another.[1]

The multitude of quote-worthy material is vast, and demonstrates the diversity with which people approach the task of curating work, no matter the medium of art. Where screendance is concerned, we as a community gather cues from the art world, from cinema, and from the world of live performance. Each have their own curatorial histories and legacies; however, like the philosophies and practices of individual curators, there exist similarities that tie these experiences together, as well as a wealth of diverse approaches specific to each genre of art. Given its hybrid nature, screendance has its very own legacies, traceable through the archives of screendance festivals past and present, and the experiences of their individual directors and curators. Thus, I believe the most salient way I can open a discourse on curating screendance is through my own experience as a screendance festival founder, director, and curator.

As I mentioned in the first chapter of this volume, I did not immediately step into the role of "curator," when I began producing a screendance festival. Like making screendance, curating is a pursuit that takes practice and the development of a set of skills and sensibilities specific to that aspiration. In the screendance community, there exist few curators who begin their careers as curators; rather, a vast majority of those who curate screendance festivals come to the practice as makers and enthusiasts first, curators second. This reality presents both challenges and advantages to the field and practice of curating screendance festivals. While the lack of formal curatorial study may mean that curators in our discipline lack an overall historical and theoretical understanding of curating as it is presented and accepted in the world of fine arts in the West, it is also true that having a lack of institutional knowledge means that

86

the journey to cultivating a practice has the potential to be more open, inspired, and informed by life experience. How many times have we seen a dancer with "no formal training" move in ways that surprise and delight us for their liberation from the rigidities of "technique" and the innovation therein?

When I held the first Movies by Movers screening in 2010 (though it was not yet called Movies by Movers), I was a graduate student. I was relatively new to my screendance practice and having had only a few experiences presenting my own work at film festivals, I was curious about the mysteries of how films were chosen for such events. The first year I curated what would become the annual Movies by Movers film festival, it was supposed to be a one-time event—a practicum project, checked off of a list of requirements as part of my work toward my Master of Fine Arts degree. I solicited films from the North Carolina dance community and, as an unknown presenter of such works, received only a handful of films in response. My first curatorial panel—a facet of the experience I included because it was something I had observed as part of the few film festivals I had thus far attended—consisted of myself, my mother, and two friends in the art community, both of whom were movers: one in dance, one in theater and yoga. We screened all the films we received except one,[2] and against my desires, we screened a film of mine too, so the show would be long enough to warrant the $10 suggested donation. As it turns out, about as many people as there were films actually came, and by the end, at least two of them were asleep! The first film on the DVD we burned flubbed and skipped; the filmmaker who had driven an hour and a half to see her film was visibly perplexed. I led a question-and-answer session with the two artists in attendance at the end of the screening, just like I had seen happen at the handful of film festivals I had previously attended. Admittedly, I didn't know enough about the films to speak about them with any depth—I hadn't done my homework to know more than was on the surface and readily visible. I can't say I was a very good moderator.

My perception of curation and programming at that time was shallow; this was *not* a curated block of films with an intentionally articulated relationship to one another. This was just a handful of movies brought together by happenstance.[3] I quickly realized that not only was the curation and presentation of films much more involved than I imagined, but that curation, programming, and producing are separate but inextricable activities that each require their own attention, while simultaneously maintaining awareness of all facets to create the scaffolding necessary to craft a successful event. That's when I decided that this practicum experiment was going to have to happen again—and this time, I needed to go deeper and do more.

The following season, I contacted the River Run Film Festival in Winston Salem, North Carolina. I approached the artistic director at the time about volunteering as an intern there. Surprisingly, he said yes. Of course, I ended up doing what interns do: I ran errands, I did data entry, I helped set up for parties and other special events, I helped with marketing, I even poured a cup of coffee or two. Leading up to the festival, I was asked by one of the staff people if I wanted to "screen any films." Not knowing what "screeners" were, I thought she was asking me to submit one of my dance films to the festival. I responded, "I would love to show you one of my dance films." To which she responded, "I'm asking if you would like to watch some of the entries. We have a few thousand and it helps to have another set of eyes." While I was not asked to rate any of the films formally, I did watch a few and give my thoughts verbally. That was a useful lesson in film festival language and a lesson in how to watch and compare films. Further, as I witnessed the screening blocks come together under various categories and overheard banter about which films should be included and why, I began to get an inkling of how one might consider the task of curating a show for an audience with the intention to do things like highlight specific themes in a collection of films, highlight aesthetic and thematic trends from specific regions of our country or the world, present retrospectives of single directors, and create generative space for new talent.

With my experience at River Run complete, I felt ready to take on the charge of curation once more. I generated a list of questions to myself:

- *Why* am I interested in presenting a collection of short screendance works to an audience?
- *Who* is my audience? *Who* are the artists I wish to attract to my call for work?
- *What* is my duty as the curator and presenter of these films? To the work? To the artists? To the audience? To the field?
- *How* does this endeavor contribute to the overall health and wellness of the field of screendance?

Soliciting dance films from the dance community once more, I opened submissions to all fifty states. I received about thirty films, and while I did not receive quite enough to make a series of separate screenings, I did have enough at least to more seriously consider the films both by their individual merits and by how they might intermingle thematically and aesthetically and be experienced by an audience in concert with each other. Again,

88

Chapter 6. Curating

I asked friends in my local arts community (no mom this time!) to act as panelists, and I shared with them my new vision for this second iteration of screenings. Finally, I decided to present a retrospective of Martha Graham's work for the screen in juxtaposition to the contemporary work I was showing. I once again approached the a/perture theater in Winston Salem, where my first screening was presented the year prior, to hold the screening. While I was proud of my growing awareness and burgeoning practice, the two screenings I held were met with mixed feelings. While people generally enjoyed the contemporary films, Martha Graham's work felt long and laborious to watch for those not in the dance community who had some prior knowledge about her and her work. I had failed to contextualize the significance of the work, and I hadn't made visible the connections I was seeing between her work and some of the works chosen for the contemporary screening. Again, I learned a lesson—that curation is as much about *creating* an experience for audiences, as it is about *contextualizing* that experience, especially where historical work is being presented. I needed to try again.

By 2012, Movies by Movers was in its third year and I was determined to continue my quest to curate and present a holistic experience of screendance. To be deemed successful by me, this event needed to fulfill four desires:

- Give an audience that would most certainly include members new to the genre a welcoming introduction to screendance.
- Communicate some definitive qualities of screendance as I was coming to know them more deeply through the work of those in the Delineator generation of screendance festival directors and curators.
- Make tangible connections between the films chosen and their shared aesthetic and thematic elements.
- Honor the individuality of practicing artists.

That year the festival moved from the a/perture to the Southeastern Center for Contemporary Art. Because there is a large screen and a stage, I was able to create a space on the program for multimedia performance—a way to help bridge the gap between totally live dance and totally digital dance. I invited three local dance companies to present their multimedia work and included a multimedia solo of my own that I choreographed on another local dancer. I also incorporated an initiative called "The Curator's Pick," a small collection of films I actively searched for on the internet and obtained permission from the artists to show as part of the events.

Screendance from Film to Festival

Because submission numbers were still low (we received about 50 submissions in 2012), I caught on to the idea that *curation is not passive*; it is an *active* endeavor that allows us as curators to shape the experience of the work intentionally. That year we screened the first feature film as part of the program and Skyped in the filmmakers from across the country for a Q&A. And, we gave out awards. There were many firsts that year, and while audience numbers remained relatively low, I still consider 2012 one of the most successful years of the festival. It was that year when the name Movies by Movers would become more than a nickname for the festival and be officially adopted. To my delight, the event was recognized as a legitimate festival by the local media, and subsequently, by myself.

Between 2013 and 2015, the festival went through more changes: the home of the festival moved from the Southeastern Center for Contemporary Art to Appalachian State University in Boone, North Carolina, in 2014, where I have been employed during the entire process of conceptualizing and writing this book. In those years, I began to curate themed screenings: LGBTQ screenings, screenings highlighting women's voices, screenings in and about nature—we did those outside in the crisp mountain air of the Appalachians with an inflatable screen and coolers of ginger ale and baskets of cookies—and more. I also stopped giving out awards, deciding that the distinction a film may receive by getting an award was outweighed by my desire to seriously consider the value of the platform and the presentation of all the films chosen as pieces of equal value to the entirety of the experience. Finally, I decided to begin acting as a single curator for the festival, curious as to why screendance festivals had panels in the first place. Is it because the volume of films makes it hard to consider all of them carefully? Is it because there is value in having many voices in the selection process? Is it because that's just the model that has been given to us? Or rather, the model we've adopted because we haven't seen another model? In addition to making the change because of curatorial quandary, I became committed to using the submission pool as a research tool to study issues of representation in screendance. Thus, my process of curation became much more time-intensive and engrossed rather than just looking at the films from a cinematic point of view. My curatorial practice has been both deepened and broadened by the extended time spent with the films and by my need to know more about dance films from multiple aspects including what's on the surface and what's not always immediately apparent.

As Movies by Movers made the transition to becoming ADF's Movies by Movers through the merging of Movies by Movers and the Dance for Camera Festival at the American Dance Festival in late 2015, my desire to more succinctly cultivate a curatorial philosophy only became stronger. I began staging installations that beg questions about our relationship to digital space and analog space. I have become more committed to curating along thematic lines, thinking more deeply about where films are shown in concert with the chosen themes of the films (site-informed and site-specific screenings), while also leaving space each festival to put together a fun, "something for everyone" collection of films. These screenings are great ways to help audiences new to screendance enter the conversation. I now think of my curatorial pursuits not only as opportunities to screen films, but also to curate a holistic event of digital and analog movement experiences upheld by my continually growing knowledge in the field and my ongoing curiosity about what makes a well-curated and well-produced event. It is worth noting that in anticipation of the 2020 season, I reinstated the use of a panel, prompted by the impending birth of my first child in late 2019 and the realization that my attention would be divided. In my need to continue to confront existential curatorial challenges, I carefully solicited the help of people who are both versed in the practice of screendance, while also having other aspects to their practices in community-engaged art, cinema, live dance, and arts education.

There are ever-present challenges to upholding the ideals that I have set forth for myself as a curator, many of which are the practical challenges of space and resources that are inherent in nearly all screendance festivals. However, as it will become apparent when I describe in more detail some of the curatorial experiments and pursuits I have undertaken, curating offers us opportunities to not only *show* what's happening in the field, but to actively *dream* about ways to engage people from across the artistic ecosystem in aesthetic experience, observe trends in screendance works for the purpose of highlighting and critiquing them, contribute to conversations about what screendance includes as time and our digital lives march on, and actively support artists and the field at large through our activism.

In keeping with this constant inquiry, I have constructed a personal treatise on curating that I'll present as a culmination to this book that I hope will function not only as an expanded expression of my own views on the matter, but as an invitation to others in the field to share widely their own philosophies, to contest my philosophy, and ultimately to deepen the pool of the discourse that exists on the subject of curating in screendance. But before that happens, and before I explain specific curatorial projects, I think it necessary to briefly explore the history and theory of curating as a practice in the Western fine arts constellation for the purpose of providing a platform from which to diverge into a broader exploration of philosophies as they exist on the screendance circuit and in the world more broadly.

Curatorial Roots in Western Culture

Curating in the arts as it is understood from a Western perspective finds its roots in pre-medieval Roman society and medieval Europe. The Latin word, *"cura,"* "to take care of," is the root word for *"curate,"* which in Roman society meant someone who might act as a guardian or steward of a specific area of civic life. For instance, one might be a caretaker for the road system, or one could be a caretaker for a minor entering into a legal contract, among other things (Balzer 2015, 30). By medieval times, the word meant someone who was a spiritual caretaker of a parish—someone whose business it was to care for the souls of others. By the 16th century, curation had taken on a very different meaning across Europe where people became gatherers and guardians of collections of cultural artifacts. *Kunstkammer,* as they were called in Germany, also called *"wonder rooms"* or *"cabinets of curiosities"* in English-speaking Europe and *"studiolo," "museo,"* and *"galleria"* in other parts of Europe, were collections of art, religious relics, antiquities, natural curiosities, and/or scientific instruments in the homes and palaces of the wealthiest members of society. These collections functioned as repositories of knowledge and helped to fashion the owners of such compendia as cultured and invested in the pursuit of the kind of worldly knowledge that separated them from common people. Owners of the artifacts included in these collections often prided themselves on their rarity or perceived novelty. The curators (often called *"keepers"*) (George 2015, 150) in charge of these collections—sometimes the owners of the collections themselves, and sometimes individuals hired for the specific purpose of overseeing the collections—were subservient to these collections such that the importance of the collection eclipsed that of the curator, whose job it was to be connoisseur, broker, protector, and docent. By the 18th century, private wonder rooms were being replaced by public museums. While these museums were in no way completely public nor separate from the political ambitions of their respective locations—gallerist Karsten Schubert described the early European museum as "the handmaiden of imperialism (Balzer 2015, 36)"—they did help to begin to shift the paradigm of how people experienced collections of objects and how curators considered their role in those experiences. Hence, the role of the curator in the 18th and 19th centuries became one of championing and aiding the work of nation-building, while at the same time contributing to the pool of public knowledge.

By the early 20th century, the definition of the curator had once again begun to shift as the museum space itself underwent various transformations. The once-cluttered, gilded facilities of the 18th and 19th centuries became clean, spacious galleries whereby art could be considered separate from the building it was housed in. Modernist works challenged previously accepted modes of display and presentation, forcing curators to begin to respond to the needs of artists to more directly involve patrons as active spectators in the work. Those who considered themselves part of the avant-garde movements of the 1910s and '20s resisted institutionalization through the development and presentation of their own exhibitions and performance events. By the mid–20th century, the curator had become somewhat of an *auteur*, a person whose influence over the exhibitions they curated was palpable enough that their presence in the exhibitions sometimes eclipsed that of the artists themselves. The 1960s and '70s marked an increase in the area of independent curation. A shift in curatorial practice to better include work that is a departure from objecthood (placing things in space) meant that curators had now become concerned with live art as an important part of the fine arts landscape. Performance art, dance, and theater helped to continue to shape museum spaces as well as specific sites and environments made especially for housing live works as the post-modern movement embraced conceptual exploration, the importance of the body as art, and ephemerality in lieu of easily-categorized pieces of object-based art. Video art also heavily influenced the practice of curating in the 1960s and '70s as this new medium literally changed the way museums and their staff thought about space, time, and how patrons might experience time-based work through encounters with new media. Shifts in the capacity of arts spaces to support video meant a reorganization of the physical space of exhibition rooms and the introduction of the aesthetic influence of new equipment that would soon become common place in museums. As the Western world saw steady economic growth following the short decline of the early 1980s, the concept of the "star curator" could be linked to arts museums' alignment with corporate ventures, the expansion of the arts market and the proliferation of biennales. The 1990s saw the development of the first educational programs and surge in scholarship dedicated to curation, further legitimizing the decidedly ambiguous field of practice.

Although more latent in its participation in the curatorial landscape given its relative age to other forms of art, cinema has gone through several curatorial eras of its own that are in some ways comparable to that of fine art. While film scholars posit that "there is still no substantial and comprehensive institutional theory of film production, distribution and exhibition (Bosma 2015, 11)," there is fodder for discussion to be found on these subjects, as demonstrated by the shear amount of cinema festivals across the world today, and the books, university programs, grant programs and more, dedicated to cinema.

Historically, curating in cinema is recognized as having begun in 1895 with the Lumiere Brothers in Paris, who offered the world the first recorded public film screening (Bosma 2015, 14).

According to cinema scholar Marijke De Valck, there are three distinct periods of film programming. The first was characterized by government officials choosing national films for screening at international film festivals. These films were meant to maintain the "good nature between nations." An obvious continuation and counterpart to the project of nation-building described in the museum realm of the 18th and 19th centuries, this period of curation would enable the proliferation of the film festival we know today. This period of curation lasted from the inception of the Venice International Film Festival in 1932 until the interruption of Cannes in 1968.

The second period of film curation was characterized by the rise and recognition of the film festival director. This person was the identity of the festival for which he (the mid–20th-century film festival circuit was quite sexist and few women and non-binary people held positions of influence) worked, and his aesthetic and philosophical leanings were highlighted in the festival. This shift was brought on by a call from the film community to individualize festivals and uphold cinephilia as a central tenet and activity of those festivals. This period lasted from 1968 until the late 1980s.

The third period of film curation came in the 1990s, where judging panels became the norm. The panels served to provide more in-depth critique of films being considered for the festivals, and also helped to further legitimize the curatorial activities of the festivals by including "industry professionals" and renowned makers on their panels. The more famous the panel, the more clout your festival had.

For all genres of art, the 21st century has brought with it a host of curatorial philosophies and practices now concerned with reimagining the definition and role of the curator in institutional spaces and the dismantling of dominant and supremacist hierarchies therein. Curating has also become ubiquitous with digital and popular culture, with influencers taking on the title to describe the collection and arrangement of everything from celebrity content to lifestyle concepts and practices. Whether or not this actually "counts" as curation has continued to spark debate between those firmly positioned in the arts world and those working in the realm of popular culture. Whether or not one agrees, this expanded definition of the word and the practice will continue to exist for years to come, if not indefinitely.

CHAPTER 7

Mapping Curatorial Development in Screendance Festivals

Though not all screendance festival directors and curators have an awareness of the trappings of curation, nor do there exist an abundance of articulated philosophies with regard to curating screendance, there are curatorial touchstones we can look to in our lineage that provide the field with information about the development of the curatorial presence in screendance. Chapter 4's discussion of the four generations of screendance gives us a place to begin to mine past festival events to find examples of intentional, sensitive curating that suggests that perhaps we have not done the work to acknowledge these contributions to the field and that varied models of curation offer us entryways into possibilities for thinking about and accomplishing this subjective task.

Hans Ulrich Obrist explains that "curating as a profession means at least four things. It means to preserve, in the sense of safeguarding the heritage of art. It means to be the selector of new work. It means to connect to art history. And it means displaying or arranging the work" (Obrist 2014).

What examples do we have of this curatorial trajectory of screendance? If we look at the causes taken up by each generation of screendance festival founders, directors, and curators, we can see that curatorial concerns shift as awareness grows over time, and as the curatorial pool becomes more and more diverse. We can see clearly that the field's curatorial concerns move from preservation, to delineation, to expansion, to breaking traditions and boundaries.

Muriel Lobl, then–Chairman of the Board of the Dance Films Association wrote in 1970, "if the motion picture is to record the total human experience, it must not overlook that most ephemeral of art forms, the dance" (Lobl 1970). A declaration of principle, this statement demonstrates the drive behind the curatorial viewpoint of the Dance Films Association and permeates both the history and current trappings of the Dance on Camera Festival, perhaps in part explaining its longevity. The recorded history of the Dance Films Association serves to provide the field of screendance with evidence of a clear intention and method behind the solicitation, collection, screening, and distribution of dance films and films on the topic of dance. Long before the inception of the annual festival, Susan Braun and her team were working to identify and archive films from around the world, educate audiences about all aspects of dance from performance to dance education, and make space for artists to grow in their craft. These requisites existed, despite the lack of a clear definition of screendance as a genre all its own that would become clear later in the chronology of screendance festivals and initiatives. In the years leading up to the establishment of the annual festival, the DFA articulated clearly its commitment to cultivating a vast, but sound collection of films that acted as "a cultural resource which preserves our dancing heritage on mylar and celluloid."[1] Additionally, the DFA established a manner of evaluating films for the purpose of maintaining a high level of quality in their curatorial and presentational work. As stated in the fall 1970 edition of Sightlines magazine, the DFA "[inaugurated] a monthly program of film evaluations, in which dance films [would] be examined and evaluated as to the quality of the dance, the quality of the photography, and the degree of success with which the motion picture achieves its purpose" (Lobl 1970). Although a broad set of criteria, this statement, coupled with the commitment to preserve dancing heritage, creates a curatorial thesis which has stood the test of time and left room for expansion as the Dance on Camera Festival has grown over its five decades of existence. The most notable curatorial precursor to the festival that demonstrates these aims is the catalogue which DFA members had access to for the purpose of renting films. The first iteration of the catalogue published in 1979[2] boasted about 500 films with later editions containing more than a thousand, each categorized according to genre, directors and choreographers, and dance companies. Also, the organization held regular screenings before the inception of the festival that put their stated values on display. For example, a 1956 press release describes an evening of dance films from countries visited by the then-nascent New York City Ballet on their fourth tour of Europe that same season. Of particular interest among the selections was a film depicting dances inspired by the movement in paintings by Degas, and a filmed rendition of *Afternoon of a Faun*. This screening followed the very first recorded screening of the then-newly-formed Dance Films Association, a screening highlighting a visit by the Royal Danish Ballet to New York City.

Early iterations of the Dance on Camera Festival show clear curatorial connections to early activities of the organization and strong correlation to the DFA's stated goals of the time. In an era where global sensibilities were more limited than they are today, Braun and her team placed high importance on sharing films from across the world, showcasing non–Western genres of dance. Over the three days of screenings at the 1975 festival, films showcasing Indonesian, Yugoslavian, Venezuelan, and African dance were screened. These films were cultivated through government entities and commercial distributers from the various countries they represented, showing the tenacity with which Braun pursued the pieces she archived and screened for audiences. Paired with these selections are films featuring modern dance pioneers like Ruth St. Denis, ballet greats like Rudolph Nureyev, and pieces that document and preserve notable works by several prominent choreographers of the time including Gus Giordano and Alvin Ailey.

By the ninth installation of the festival, a move to include a broader range of types of films is evident. A greater number of experimental and avant-garde pieces are included in the lineup of the 1980 festival, as well as films from the dance therapy community, jazz and tap dance communities, and a continued, strong presence by non–Western dance forms.

As the festival has weathered the generational shifts of screendance festivals, the curatorial objectives of the festival have changed over time to remain current, while retaining a commitment to preservation through retrospectives and other historical programming dedicated to keeping the history of screendance and dance more broadly, alive. Following Braun's death in 1995 and the subsequent leadership of the organization by Virginia Brooks, Deirdre Towers, and Ron Honsa, the late 1990s and early 2000s saw the festival embrace many of the principles of the Delineator generation, even inspiring the formation of several of the notable festivals among the growing constellation of screendance festivals today. Beginning in 2018, the Dance on Camera Festival has continued to move with the times, incorporating digital/social media curation and has in some ways fallen in line with some of the aims of the Collectivist generation, though there exist remarkable differences which will become evident in the following paragraphs.

The Delineator generation was the first generation to take up curation as an articulated concern of the screendance festival. Spearheaded in part by Douglas Rosenberg of the Dancing on Camera Festival at the American Dance Festival (1996–2015), Rosenberg identified the endeavor as a "director's festival" and through his pursuits encouraged a greater attention to curation across the field:

Dance for Camera co-curator Liz Wolff, choreographer/dancer Robbie Fairchild and filmmaker Bat-Sheva Guez at the Dance on Camera Festival in New York City in 2019. Courtesy Dance Films Association.

While each jury defines its own particular esthetic, it is the tradition of this festival to look for work that extends the metaphors of dance into a new filmic space. In that transition from "live" to screen, the jury looks for work that redefines and questions the language of dance while also interrogating the nature of the moving image and its relationship to dance. In short, the jury looks for that ineffable gestalt in which the whole is not only greater than the sum of its parts, but the parts are also transformed in the process. In the production of media, it is the director whose eye defines what we see. And while screendance is a collaborative art, there is one privileged point of view in the making of a film. It is through the camera's lens that the meta-dance is built shot by shot, frame by frame. This method of construction is further articulated in the editing process. However, the accretion of danced moments as they are unearthed and cataloged, archived and arranged, is the territory of the director. And while the choreographer and director may be one and the same, a set of outside eyes, an alternative esthetic, and a pre-existing relationship with the medium of film or video can often unearth something nascent or germinal in the dance [Doug Rosenberg, Open Source 2006, p. 62].

Other screendance festival directors and curators from the Delineator generation took up the opportunity to deepen curatorial practice and produced the storied festival events that have helped to influence our understanding of screendance festival history and continue to make waves in the broader screendance community.

The archives of the University of Utah International Screendance Festival, founded and directed by Ellen Bromberg since 1999, demonstrate the goal of the Delineator generation to not only introduce audiences to the canon of screendance, but also to help define the genre through their efforts. The 1999 festival included two evenings of screenings that were international in scope. Films that presented the canon of screendance, including *A Study of Choreography for the Camera,* directed by Maya Deren, *Merce by Merce by Paik Part One: Blue Studio*, directed by Charles Atlas, *Dance in the Sun*, directed by Shirley Clarke, and *Dance Nine*, directed by Doris Chase, demonstrated the genre's connections to experimental film and video art movements of the mid–20th century. In addition, the screenings showed the breadth of practice by known and upcoming practitioners of the time, helping to shape the audience's understanding of the trajectory of the art from. Artists like Bridget Murnane, Douglas Rosenberg, Victoria Marks, and others were represented. The filmic work of well-known choreographers like Bill T. Jones demonstrated screendance's connections to concert dance. This program as a whole aptly revealed screendance's hybrid existence, as articulated by the Delineator generation. As part of the festival, a two-day video-dance workshop was presented by Bromberg and guest artist Doug Rosenberg. By the second year of the festival, clear curatorial statements appeared and the screenings echoed a more pointed expression of the values of those presenting festivals in the Delineator generation. The 2000 iteration of the festival was described in this way:

> In its second year, the Dance for Camera Film and Video Festival presents a tremendous diversity of dance that has been created or reconceived specifically for the screen. Each work presented has been selected either for its historic importance, its innovative use of the medium of film or video, its expansion of our definitions of dance, or for its provocative or poetic reflection of the human experience.
>
> Part of the beauty and poignancy of live dance performance is its ephemeral nature. Inherent in the very instant of a gesture is its loss, as if embodying our own temporality. While film or video can never replace the live experience, these media offer us more lasting images of what moves us, and what results from those impulses to move. A hybrid art form, Dance for the Camera combines the language of film and the language of dance, allowing for a more extended gesture in time [Bromberg 2000].

An evening dedicated to Anna Sokolow was among the highlights that year, as was a screening titled *Images of Men Dancing*, of which Bromberg

Ellen Bromberg, founding director of the University of Utah International Screendance Festival. Courtesy Ellen Bromberg.

stated, "I felt that the films themselves asked to be programmed that way!" The screening included diverse representations of men dancing, engaging a variety of concepts from the AIDS crisis, to toxic masculinity (though that term had not yet been popularly adopted), and aging.

The 2002 festival featured a collaboration with the University of Utah Gender Studies program and included a symposium. The entire event was titled *The Projected Self: Bodies, Genders, and Dance on Screen.* This iteration of the festival took the opportunity to "examine how methods of framing and editing the moving body influence our perceptions of masculinity and femininity, as well as another and perhaps a more important issue is how power relations between genders are communicated through these techniques."

This festival marks the first time in recorded screendance festival history where representation relating to gender was explored so deeply in a public event. As part of the festival that year, a retrospective of the work of Victoria Marks was presented, as well as the various workshops that have been a staple of each year of the festival since its inception. One main feature of the festivals of the Delineator generation is the celebration of each other's work as a curatorial pursuit, which in turn has helped to solidify the canon from the 1990s and onward.

Screendance from Film to Festival

Taking the reins from the Delineator generation, the Hyper-Localist generation of screendance festival directors and curators began a kind of curatorial expansion that continued to help define screendance as a genre, but also created new identity and philosophy-based pockets of programming that supported (and continue to support) a greater diversity of projects. The San Francisco Dance Film Festival, which had its first screenings in 2010, demonstrates a clear trajectory from the screening of a mixed handful of films that fall more in line with Delineator sensibilities to a robust collection of concept and subject-specific screenings over a decade later.

In 2010, the festival, a single screening with no intention of becoming a full-fledged festival (a recurring theme found among screendance festivals!), boasted just twenty films, mostly from the United States. Mitchell Rose—a maker, educator, and curator whose work is most associated with that of the Delineator generation—had two films on the program: *Advance*, which demonstrated his signature style of hyper match cutting through the depiction of a non-stop journey by two dancers through multiple locations, and *Modern Daydreams: Part One*, which exhibited Rose's fanciful conceptual sensibilities as a man dances with construction machinery. Other makers included Mouvment Perpetuél's Marlene Millar and Philip Szporer with their film, *A Soft Place to Land,* an exploration of the dynamics of romantic relationships. Twelve of the twenty films were made by California-based artists, demonstrating a strong commitment to local makers. Stand-outs among those California-based works include Mimi Cave's colorful film, *Lello,* winner of the Audience Choice Award. Greta Schonberg, the founder and first curator of the SFDFF, had a film on the program as well—a common occurrence among first film festival screenings. As a whole, the program came to just under 100 minutes, all films screened on the same program. Taken together, the films presented an impressive introduction to the festival as a budding institution and to the genre of screendance as it was being practiced between 2000 and 2010.

As the festival grew, we can observe areas where the curation breaks away from that of the previous generations, showing more diversity on screen, accepting types of films that may not have been considered screendance by the Delineator generation—such as music videos, filmed performances (which were common to Preservationist festivals), and promotional material—as well as creating curatorial teams for specific areas of festival programming. As one of the largest festivals on the American screendance festival circuit (most festivals show between

25 and 50 films each season; the SFDFF screened more than twice that amount in 2019), the selective curation of SFDFF is as much a necessity as it is a way of being intentional about how films are chosen with regard to the intended impact of the screenings they are chosen to be a part of.

The tenth anniversary festival season included well over one hundred films from across the world, organized into screenings such as "Women on the Move, A unique collection of female-directed films that brings to light the many facets of womanhood." "Raising Voices: Social Justice" saw "choreographers and filmmakers bring[ing] social justice issues to the forefront and giv[ing] voice to the under-represented artists." "Finding Me: Documentary Shorts" brought "people from all walks of life [to] explore their unique identities through dance in this inspiring collection of documentary shorts" (San Francisco Dance Film Festival, 2019). The specificity of these screenings and others can be found as manifestations of curatorial consideration among the festival offerings throughout the seasons of the SFDFF.

Included among the thirteen shorts programs is a screening of seventeen shorts by Bay Area artists, demonstrating a continued commitment to local artists. Many of these screenings included either discussions with the artists, special panels dedicated to more deeply exploring socio-cultural themes present in the films, or live performances to augment the film material. In sum, the SFDFF is effective in contextualizing the work for their audiences. Looking deeper into the selections, it is clear that the curatorial team takes an active approach to creating cohesive programs, with 15 percent of the films screened at the 2019 festival solicited outside of the submission pool. Indeed, this is a higher percentage of solicited or acquired films than most screendance festivals. Of curating, founder Greta Schonberg says, "I always try to step back from my own thinking once I've gone through all the films, and I have my own gut reactions on things.... And then I try to create a real mixture. We have a balance of things from all walks of life."

Today's Collectivist festivals show clear objectives with regard to curating, ones that are in fact the very festivals themselves. As mentioned in Chapter 4, the Mobile Dance Film Festival founded and directed by Andrew Chapman places importance on films created using mobile devices. As the popularity of small screens continues to rise and their presence becomes more ubiquitous in our lives as a whole, the art world at large has embraced their existence with numerous exhibitions and initiatives with the use of mobile devices as a curatorial jumping-off point. The inaugural festival featured twenty-four short films from eleven countries. Many of the films were created for the express purpose of submitting to the festival. And while critics questioned the overall merit of the films (Seibert 2018), the creation of a space where new films created in accessible ways are selected for screening in a live festival format is a bold move. It forces audiences and makers to contend with the question of what comprises filmic art worthy of celebration in such a format, while supporting artists in taking risks with work that does not require the financial investment that making more traditional pieces requires. In sum, a festival like this one lends itself to experimentation on the part of the artists and opens the door to creative curating that may include pieces that would otherwise not have a place on the festival circuit.

Another example of a festival-as-thesis is the Dare to Dance in Public Festival directed by Sarah Elgart. As described in Chapter 5, the Dare to Dance in Public Festival sets specific parameters around what kinds of films it is looking for:

> Dance that happens outside of stages and studios … dance that is bursting out like flowers from a cracked sidewalk … short films that explore the intersection of dance and the camera, films that spread the wealth of dance and challenge the notion that there is a proper time and place to dance. Dare to Dance in Public Film Festival begs the question: *Why can't dance happen anywhere … at any time?*

Although the festival invites films made by any number of methods, the festival receives several pieces filmed on mobile devices each season in addition to several pieces created specifically for the purpose of submitting to the festival. The public nature of the films as dictated by the festival thesis means that the films selected as part of the festival often have a guerrilla-type quality to them. Again, a platform like this supports artists in accessible filmmaking and experimentation that some of the more traditional festivals may not support as readily.

Gabri Christa's Moving Body–Moving Image Festival sets forth specific aims in its curation that highlight specific groups in ways not often seen on the circuit. The first iteration of the festival launched in 2018 featured "The Brown Body in Screendance." The second iteration held in 2020 (this is a bi-annual festival) is all about "The Aging Body in Screendance." Both of these events will be more thoroughly addressed in the chapters on representation. Because of the focused nature of the festival, films are both solicited through submissions and acquired through active collection.

104

Chapter 7. Mapping Curatorial Development

As discussed in Chapter 5 as well, Film Fest by Rogue Dancer creates online and live space for themed screenings throughout the year. The acquisition of the films is both active, with festival director Jennifer Scully-Thurston reaching out directly to filmmakers to gain permission to include their works, as well as a rolling submissions process that is cheap and accessible to a wide range of artists.

All four of these Collectivist-era festivals demonstrate how a more-focused approach to curating screendance creates space for new experiments and diversifies the assemblage of pieces seen across the landscape of screendance festivals. It is an important feature of these festivals that they often feature films not found anywhere else on the circuit.

As we recognize our curatorial past and present, perhaps it isn't so much about the *what* of curating, but the *how*. We can no longer be mired in the task of finding one definition of curating that suits the field as a whole, nor a singular approach to curating, rather we should be engaged in asking questions about how our own respective practices, in their diversity and in their commonalities, are contributing to the health of the field. Is the health and survival of the field not the driving force behind our endeavors as space is made to screen films as well as host workshops, forge academic programs, coordinate symposia and conferences, publish written scholarship, and facilitate opportunities for screendance artists to meet in space and make new work? As demonstrated by the trajectory of screendance's history, curatorial evolution has and continues to take place as new iterations and configurations of the screendance festival emerge. It is quite possible, given the ramifications of the Covid-19 pandemic, that new types and approaches to festival-making will emerge in the years to come as the art world grapples with the long-term hurdles created by the pandemic. So maybe the conversation around curating isn't so much about helping screendance to develop or articulate a philosophy and practice that doesn't exist. Instead, it could be about acknowledging our history and current events to illuminate and articulate an *already-existing* trajectory of curating in the field, recognizing that each notable development in curatorial practice is one informed by socio-cultural awareness as it pertains to various eras, place, resources, and screendance's own development and visibility in the public sphere.

In some ways, screendance has moved faster than other art forms with longer histories. As screendance festivals across the world share material and are deeply connected by both personal and digital relationships, works of screendance are being taken up by various curators in different contexts. This is important because it clues us into the possibilities of programming, juxtaposition, and synergy between works while pro-viding information about the specific curatorial concerns of each festival team. With the expansion of the screendance festival, we can readily see how works of screendance can be recontextualized from space to space. This may be a way of looking at the field as a site of meta-curation, where looking at the landscape as a whole as opposed to analyzing individual fes-tivals may give us insight into how works are perceived conceptually, cine-matically and choreographically across diverse groups of people. As a site of meta-curation, the screendance festival landscape can and does serve as a space where definitions are being redefined each season with the sup-port of voices coming from different artistic and aesthetic schools and experiences.

In the end, the most important aspect of this conversation to me seems to be the process of uncovering what exists for the purpose of finding and illuminating diverse perspectives and practices moving forward, recogniz-ing that each one offers us information about what's being made in the field and how people are meeting and consuming it.

In mining and articulating the curatorial lineages and histories of screendance festivals, it seems the most important part of that is *telling the story of the festival*. Many festivals conclude each season with no more archive than a list of films, some program notes, some photographs and a few reels. After a festival has concluded its season, I want to know what the dynamic was among those on the curatorial team and how did they ultimately choose the lineup for the festival? What films forced the cura-tors to come to a standstill in their deliberations? Who was at the festi-val who were not featured artists, presenters, or organizers? What were their takeaways from the festival? What conversations about the work took place in between scheduled events? Between whom? What was the most talked-about film, workshop, or panel? Why? Which artists hit it off and have set off on a new collaborative journey? Who was the most enthusiastic audience member? What was their most poignant ques-tion during the artist talk-back? How did the artist answer? What parts of the festival are sticking in peoples' minds, weeks after the festival has concluded? It is important that these details are not lost so that the world can begin to have a clearer picture of what screendance festivals are all about and how curatorial decisions influence the overall experience of a festival.

As a way of contributing to what I hope is a burgeoning collection of stories of the screendance festival, I offer the next chapter as an expli-cation of my adventures in curating. Specific events are explored and the ethos around those events is presented with as much importance as the works themselves. It is idealistic, but I hope that readers take the next chapter as an invitation to other curators, artists, and audience members to begin preserving their own adventures in screendance and screendance festivals.

CHAPTER 8

Curatorial Adventures

Adventure, as it is described in the dictionary, is a remarkable and/or exciting experience, one that often also includes an element of risk or danger. Screendance festivals hardly seem like spaces where the threat of any real danger exists, but the task of introducing audiences to work they've never seen before can be risky given the very real implications of stagnant audience development for many festivals. The presentation of known or more mainstream work in new ways also welcomes risks, where the reward of reframing an accepted cultural narrative, for example, can be a powerful occurrence that keeps the field fresh and forward-looking.

Excitement is easy to come by in the curatorial process if we are curious, engaged, and committed to the work. Excitement is the sentiment we hope our audiences feel when they attend our events, among other feelings that may include intrigue, fascination, delight, and connection. Artists should also feel excitement as they think about how their work will be cared for and presented in our festivals. It is true, we don't always get it right, but that risk is often outweighed by the feeling you get when an event has gone well and all parties involved have been addressed with as much consideration as possible. I describe my curatorial pursuits as adventures because I do find them to be exciting and challenging parts of my work in screendance. As demonstrated through the mining of our curatorial histories and developments in screendance in previous chapters, curators of screendance festivals can play important parts in framing our collective understanding of the field, of our culture, and of our social and intellectual contexts in the broader world of the arts.

As a practice, my curatorial style is interrogative. It is a mixture of passive receipt and active mining for material, asking how the work can best be shown, and engaging with artists to create new and interesting experiences. Ultimately, I wish for the audience to interact deeply with the work in ways that are informed by our collective social and cultural experiences in the 21st century. I want everyone involved—artists, audiences, and presenters—to be engaged in the exchange of cultural capital, that is, the acquisition of knowledge and awareness through shared cultural experiences. By investigating ways that we can take advantage of the social and intellectual currency I've described, we can steer the narrative about screendance and its future. Thus, this chapter is a small collection of curatorial projects I describe for the purpose of demonstrating the kind of activism in screendance (part and parcel with my work in representation described in Chapters 9 and 10) that makes it a dynamic field with goals of accessibility, inviting new audiences to the form, and accentuating the creative, intellectually stimulating, and social atmosphere that is indicative of screendance and other independent film genres. Some of these endeavors have taken place within the context of ADF's Movies by Movers, others have taken shape independently as opportunities to construct special exhibitions and events. All of the activities described have contributed to my overall understanding of the implications of my curatorial pursuits, and how to continue growing my capacity to creatively engage the field as but one attendant of screendance platforms.

* * *

In September 2017, I launched ADF's Movies by Movers' first-ever mini-exhibition. My goal in this exhibition was to create an intimate, interactive experience working within the boundaries of a limited space made available to me through the university where I currently teach. The HOW Space—now called the Walker WORKspace—is a multi-purpose building leased by the College of Business at Appalachian State University and exists in a heavily-trafficked area of town. The building has two spaces—a larger gallery and maker's space that is most often used for large class exhibitions, class meetings, college-wide events and special workshops, and a much smaller front room with a very large picture window that looks out onto the sidewalk. I was to be situated in this smaller space. In seeking to bridge the worlds of embodied experience and viewing screendance, I asked a handful of American artists to create collections of photographs for stop-motion flipbooks that people could hold and manipulate with their own hands. These "dances in your hands" as I called them, coupled with a collection of one-minute films on iPads placed around the room, gave people options for ambulating around the space and being active in their watching experience. People seemed to love the flipbooks most, having the power to control the speed and direction (forward or backward) of the dances they held. With our almost exclusively digital understanding of media in the 21st century, the opportunity to experience movement through analog expressions helped to remind audiences of how far we've come in our technology, what our expectations of those technologies are, and how we got there. For many of the college students that attended the exhibition, the flipbooks were an entirely new experience that garnered spontaneous exclamations like "Oh, cool!" and "This is so dope!" Additionally, there was the novelty of choosing the order in which to watch the tiny films on the iPads that inspired conversation among patrons of the exhibition. People compared watching the mini-film collection to experiencing a full music album—also a rare occurrence in the 21st century—with the energetic experience of the collection of works influenced by the order one saw them in. Placing the looping iPads in the windows for people walking to nearby bars, restaurants and shops in the evenings after the HOWSpace closed expanded the exhibition out onto the street. Passersby stopped and stood close to the window to observe the moving media before heading the rest of the way to their destinations. Many lingered for several minutes, long enough to watch all of the films. Some returned to the space over the weekend to come inside and experience the whole exhibition. For those to whom screendance was unfamiliar, the exhibition seemed to give many an experience that demonstrated to them what screendance is and could be without the anxiety of being "trapped" in a theater for ninety minutes, "not knowing what to expect." For some audience members, the exhibition acted as a gateway to the more traditional screenings included in the festival, lifting the veil of mystery as to what makes a screendance, a screendance, and why they are enjoyable to watch.

The visibility of the exhibition meant that the work enjoyed greater viewership than films screened only once or twice over the course of the festival. The final facet of this exhibition was the creation of a community dance film, an idea I borrowed from the DanceBARN Festival in Battle Lake, Minnesota. The creation of other community dance film works has also been seen at festivals like the Portland Dance Film Festival and the Sans Souci Festival of Dance Cinema. My goal in creating the community dance film was to introduce people to screendance in an interactive way, in keeping with the mini-exhibition, and to raise the visibility of the festival. The evening the community dance film was produced, people from all walks of life stopped at our filming station and provided the project with original movements and poses, as well as suggestions for how subsequent passersby could participate in the project. In total, 24 people opted to appear on camera, with several more co-directing their friends from off-camera. The community dance film was shared across social media platforms and through Appalachian State University communication platforms.

Cara Hagan at ADF's Movies by Movers in 2018. Photo by Robert Gelber.

With the success of the mini-exhibition in 2017, I wanted to continue to find ways to push the boundaries of the festival platform while creating opportunities for interaction and increased socio-cultural accessibility in 2018. I decided to take to social media. Instagram is a social media platform founded in 2010 by developers Kevin Systrom and Mike Krieger that was originally meant to be a platform for sharing photographs only. In 2013, the service launched video-sharing capabilities, beginning with just 15-second videos, soon expanding to allow for one-minute videos. Since the expansion to accommodate one-minute videos, many have used the platform to create original material specifically for that space, share promotional material, share snippets of larger digital works, and to play. In February 2018, just after FilmFreeway submissions closed in preparation for ADF's Movies by Movers' 2018 season, I launched ADF's Movies by Movers' first-ever Instafest using the hashtags #mbminstafest and #oneminutemovie. Wondering where there might exist other such celebrations of creative work using Instagram as the central platform for sharing and viewing, I searched the hashtags #instafest and #instafestival across Instagram. I found that the vast majority of these tags are referring to pictures and video taken *at* festivals (of all kinds) instead of media uploaded to Instagram with Instagram *being* the festival platform. With questions concerning concepts of place and the creation of digital communities in my mind, I was able to use the Instafest as a space to foster a global collection of works made by professional artists, emerging artists, amateur artists, and movers who may not even identify themselves as artists. I wanted to create a space where anyone could visit and leave with new ideas of what constitutes a "festival" or a "screendance" and who and what kind of work can be included in that.

To have makers participate in the #mbminstafest, users were encouraged to tag @adfsmoviesby, the ADF's Movies by Movers Instagram username, in their favorite videos featuring movement of all kinds including dance, cirque, skating, parkour, surfing, ice skating, synchronized swimming, performance art, and more, so that they could be reposted. Of the collection that coalesced on the page, about half were acquired through tagging by the artists who would like their work shared, and about half were acquired by me simply asking the makers if they would allow me to repost their work. There were, of course, a good number of movies that would readily be described as "dance films" by the dance film community. Others were indicative of the many one-off, largely unplanned videos found across Instagram meant to highlight new dance combinations, show off cool tricks and moves by athletes and performers, and to self-promote. Others existed in an in-between space, where people have created movies featuring movement that is slowed down, sped up, rendered in black and white, or other simple edits that make the experience of the movement one that could not be experienced in real life, yet the work is not organized or polished to the degree of many of the projects reposted by self-described screendance makers. The Instafest continued on Instagram until June 23, 2018, the beginning of the festival in physical space at the American Dance Festival. Like curating for more traditional festival screenings, the curatorial process for the Instafest was a multifaceted endeavor.

Following the close of the Instafest, I constructed an installation featuring many of the films reposted as part of the Instafest. This tiny exhibition titled the "Insta-Lation" was installed at the Turchin Center for the Visual Arts in September 2018 on a collection of monitors. My intention for the Insta-Lation was to highlight art made on platforms like Instagram in ways that help both audiences and artists to reconsider what "fine art" or art worthy of a film festival includes. I wanted to share some of the sophisticated, innovative works of art found through a platform where such things appear and disappear quickly as newsfeeds refresh each moment with new material. My hope with expanding the Instafest to include the exhibition was to provide artists with varied audiences in both digital and live space for work that is made with resources and equipment more widely available to the population than professional equipment, such as smart phones and free apps. My ultimate goal in straddling the worlds of the digital and live space is to help keep the conversation about what screendance can be going, while encouraging artists to keep experimenting with creative ways of engaging 21st-century digital platforms by amplifying their efforts.

Keeping in mind my aforementioned goals of accessibility, inclusivity, and harnessing the social and creative currency of screendance, one finds that 2018 and 2019 offered yet more opportunities to curate unique experiences for new and seasoned audiences alike.

One of my long-time dreams has been to construct a screendance booth, much like the nickelodeons of the early 20th century. In July 2018, I had the pleasure of working with the DanceBARN Festival in Battle Lake, Minnesota, to realize this dream of mine. The booth, constructed from a repurposed telephone booth, was set at the edge of a sidewalk downtown during one of the busiest tourist weekends of the summer. The booth contained a collection of tiny films (between 45 seconds and four minutes) created by an international group of screendance artists. The works varied

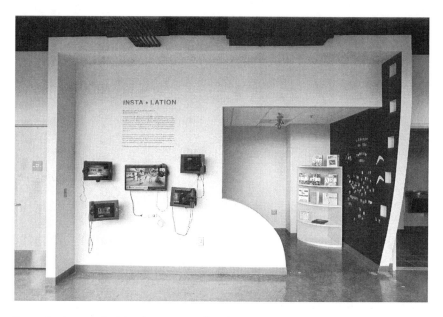

Insta-Lation at the Turchin Center for the Visual Arts in Boone, North Carolina, in 2018. Courtesy Craig Dillenbeck, Turchin Center for the Visual Arts.

in scope, from one-minute iPhone films to high production value festival films. Curious as it was sitting in the middle of a busy sidewalk, the booth was well frequented and I had the pleasure of popping in at times to explain the installation to people who would not consider themselves dance enthusiasts, much less screendance aficionados. The most fun aspect of having the booth installation was watching people speculate about what they thought was in the booth before taking their turn to go in. "Screendance?" I would hear pedestrians exclaim. Inside the booth, I left a box with a small opening for people to put in donations intended for the artists whose work was featured in the booth. And while there was not much cash to speak of by the end of the weekend, the booth still felt like a success—a very public, accessible, fun screendance installation outside of the parameters of the film festival that fulfilled one of my long-held curatorial dreams, one I hope to repeat again in various cities as opportunities become available.

In the spring and summer of 2019, I had the opportunity to mount another exhibition outside of the realm of the festival. During the fall of 2018, I began the process of preparing to curate a full-scale exhibition in

Cara Hagan putting the finishing touches on her screendance booth in Battle Lake, Minnesota, in 2018. Photo by Robert Gelber.

The screendance booth in downtown Battle Lake, Minnesota, 2018. Photo by Cara Hagan.

the vein of a philosophy I myself had been working on since the year prior. "Artistic surrogacy" is a method of sharing artistic concepts through performances, presentations, experiences, and objects which are shared, in that one person's (or several persons') ideas are placed in the hands of another (or a group) to be executed with care in the absence of the originator(s). While choreography is like this—where dancers are the vessel of the choreographer—artistic surrogacy is different, in that the work can take place between people of different training, even different artistic genres. The goal of artistic surrogacy is to find creative ways of embodying and bringing to life work that is not inherently yours, with respect to differences in demographic, culture, training, and geography of the collaborators. In essence, artistic surrogacy is a way of transmitting ideas across borders, across bodies, in ways that uphold the core values of the work, while leaving room for translational growth.

For this exhibition, titled *My Place or Yours?*, artists working across great distances, many of whom have never met in person, created new, multifaceted works together. In addition to works in photography, fiber, paper, and other media, several works included screendance. One work in particular that stood out for its depth and relationship to the practice of screendance was Julie Iarisoa's *A Trip Around My Navel,* a piece created in response to poet Elizabeth Meade's poem, "What Happened to My Legs," which describes her experience of losing the use of her legs due to cerebral palsy as a teenager. As part of the literature for the exhibition catalogue, the artists describe why such a collaboration was impactful for them, and how these particular mediums of art allow their ideas to travel, even when they themselves cannot.

Julie Iarisoa wrote:

> As a Malagasy living in Madagascar, traveling is a luxury, even to go from one city to another … and to travel to another country is almost a whole year's salary without counting the difficult steps to obtain a visa even to visit a country among the African continent…. I therefore allow myself to travel through my desires and my soul as it is still accessible … a trip around my navel….
>
> The reason why I still exist as a free and independent woman artist today is that I still allow myself to live free, to want, to think and to dream … everyday I'm fighting for living instead of just surviving because to give up life is to accept to die at small or high fire.

Elizabeth Meade writes:

> As someone who gets around by wheelchair, travel (even a road trip) is something I cherish and don't get to do as much as I would like because of the cost and accessibility. It isn't the same, but this makes me quite familiar with travel "around the navel." There's something about being in one spot that forced me to pay attention to detail and live passionately in the present moment. My mother was from Cameroon. I sometimes wonder what my life would look like if I were born there instead of the U.S., though I probably wouldn't have survived in an African hospital back then…."

Their work across continents and oceans demonstrates the capacity for screendance to transcend geographical space and offer collaborative terrain that is generative and creates avenues by which marginalized voices can be heard.

Another notable work from *My Place or Yours?* is by American artist Jocelyn Moser and Mexican artist Cinthia Perez Navarro. Again, working in disparate geographical spaces, the films included in their collaborative piece depict a conversation between two people where they begin to know each other as artists and as women. Their conversation, in both Spanish and English, yielded a small zine for display in the gallery, as well as a collection of three dance films where Cinthia dances in various spaces around Cholula, Mexico, where she is based and an active member of the contact improvisation and contemporary dance communities. Perez Navarro

Film still from Julie Iarisoa's dance film, *A Trip Around My Navel,* **at Revolve Gallery in Asheville, North Carolina, as part of the** *My Place or Yours?* **exhibition, 2019. Photo by Cara Hagan.**

dances atop a roof, in a studio, and in a field next to a busy street to musical scores composed by Moser, who is a musician. The scores feature recordings of both women's voices incorporated. At the opening of the exhibition, Moser closes the loop by recording ambient sound and the voices of patrons who visit her temporary, durational sound installation for the purpose of sending mixes of those recordings back to Perez Navarro as she could not attend the opening, living so far away from North Carolina.

Finally, the work by American dance and visual artist Suzanne Ostersmith and Irish film artist Deirdre O'Toole featured the opportunity for tactile engagement. In the middle of the gallery in the Turchin Center hung a set of flowing hand-painted fabric panels designed and created by Ostersmith. After walking through the fabric pieces, one lands upon a screen with a work directed by O'Toole that features a group of dancers, Ostersmith included among them. Ostersmith choreographed the movement for the film. Based on the topic of drowning, the fabric and film provided patrons with a gripping, engaging experience that linked cinematic and embodied experience demonstrating yet another creative way that screendance can be conceived of and enjoyed outside of a theater.

The opportunity to curate *My Place or Yours?* in particular gave me a chance to explore and share the ways screendance can move across space and geography to create intimate experiences. The thesis for this show was strong and the outcome was poignant. It illustrated the magic that can happen when you give artists a prompt and let them do what they do best! When we put our minds to it, we can all create adventures that speak to what makes screendance so special.

Despite all the magic that can be experienced during the curatorial process, I don't think any screendance festival director or curator would call the job easy. The reality of curating any screendance event is that there are many moving parts, and often it takes a tremendous amount of work to make all the pieces fit.

CHAPTER 9

Investigating Representation as Curatorial Activism

If it is the role of the curator to care for the material that constitutes the screendance landscape, it is the duty of the curator to understand the power they possess, to influence the perception audiences have of the work and to influence the trajectory of the field at large. When a patron arrives to a festival to view a block of films, they come to that experience informed by what they think they already know about what they're going to see, their own worldview, and the sensibilities and precedents imparted to them by screendance festivals in the collective (if they frequent screendance festivals) and mainstream visual culture. Similarly, when artists submit their films or are invited to have their projects included in festivals, their understanding of the context of their work in the larger landscape of screendance is informed by the trends and patterns observable across festivals, their experiences of the conversations around their works that happen during festivals (which are inevitably informed by the worldview of those taking part in the conversations), and their own experiences as audience members viewing work that is not their own. In fact, when artists go about the task of making work, they may very well be thinking about the ways that their work will fit into the panorama of the screendance festival circuit, given what material they see privileged across festivals. In some cases, this may have real influence over what gets made. It is not only possible but provable that the way festivals are curated influences who assumes their work is a good fit and therefore submits or accepts invitations to have their work screened at these events. Moreover, it is not only possible but provable that the way festivals are curated influences how people understand definitions of screendance and what is included under that umbrella. Looking at it this way, the role of curating is more than just a philosophical undertaking. Curators have a responsibility to the field to be conscientious of how their curatorial decisions affect the field, and how their understanding of who is seen on screen, who isn't seen on screen, how people are seen on screen, who is making the films, who is watching the films, and who is choosing the films implies a value system that can be attributed to the field but that may or may not be held by everyone in the field.

Therefore, it is incumbent upon those who identify as part of the curatorial community in screendance to be actively engaged in a practice of awareness-building around issues of representation in the field. I like to think of this pursuit as a form of activism that has the health and well-being of the field in mind, as well as the well-being of the artists whom we seek to uplift through the celebration of screendance.

In initiating a discussion about how representation is experienced in screendance festivals, I wish to more explicitly situate myself as a practitioner, philosopher, and researcher in this instance. In the first chapter of this book, I mentioned that my desire to dance professionally was inspired in part by the movie musicals of the Golden Age of Hollywood. What I didn't say in that chapter is that in these films I rarely saw myself—a mixed-race, Black girl—represented. The images I *did* see of women of color, especially Black women, were informed by stereotype and exoticization. If I did see Black or Brown female dancers of color who were depicted in innocuous ways, but not the absolute center of attention, their presence often went uncredited and was therefore rendered as incidental parts of the filmic landscape. White women, on the other hand, were held up as the epitome of beauty and grace, a standard by which all women were, and still are, expected to adhere in American culture.

Growing up in dance, I was fortunate to receive much of my early instruction at a Black-owned dance studio, attended by mostly Black and Brown girls. While this was a formative experience, it did not insulate me from the realities of dance as a field, where whiteness, youth, thinness, and unfettered ability are prized. I have experienced racism and sexism in all spaces where I practice dance: while performing, in academic spaces, on the job market, at conferences, and in the studio while practicing. The way my body and my art is perceived by those in the field has had very real implications for which spaces I have been allowed to occupy creatively, what types of movement are most expected and accepted to come from my body, and how I am received when I seek funding and other support for my work. Segregation in dance is often born of unconscious bias and assumptions about what "good technique" includes, what forms of dance are considered more valuable than others, what makes someone and their movement "beautiful," and who holds the power to grant space, funds, and visibility. The dance field continues to grapple with its history of aesthetic hierarchy and the erasure of the contributions of marginalized dance practitioners. Film remains embroiled in its own controversies over representation. Screendance is no exception. Although through my experience I have necessarily been most concerned with race and binary constructions of gender, expanded definitions of gender identity, ability, and age are also important pieces of the representational puzzle.

It is helpful to reiterate here that the inception of the screendance festival was largely divorced from socio-political impetus, unlike other specialized film festivals like women's film festivals, LGBTQIA+ film festivals, disability film festivals, and Black film festivals. While those festivals were working to use their platforms to help marginalized filmmakers, their stories, and their struggles for civil rights receive more attention and to more meaningfully break into the film industry, screendance was working to define itself. The lack of expediency and the notion that overall visibility could be delayed for nurturing the form speaks to a level of privilege that screendance festivals by and large did not and do not exist a matter of declaring the humanity of the community they represent. Further, it assumes there was and is time to banter and to philosophize as there were and are resources enough to keep the community going. Although finances available to screendance makers and festivals are meager as compared to other genres of filmmaking overall, the community clearly includes those able to create, submit, and program work despite that hurdle. Those who have or can find access to the resources to make work and mount festivals enjoy a privileged place in the field with increased visibility and literature dedicated to their efforts. And although there are overlaps among the film communities mentioned above—there is no shortage of women screendance makers, and there exist many queer, Black, Brown, and Crip screendance makers—certainly, the continued insulation of screendance speaks the loudest when considering matters of representation.

When I first entered the field of screendance in 2007, I did not see myself represented in the vast majority of pieces I saw, nor did I see myself represented in the pool of gatekeepers which included curators, funders, and commentators on the form. As a further point of context, it is necessary to mention that to my knowledge I am the first Black woman in the United States to be the sole founder of a screendance festival. As mentioned in Chapter 4 on the four generations of screendance festival directors, Lenwood Sloan is most likely the first Black man to initiate a screendance festival in the United States and it is telling that there have been so few screendance festival founders of color between the inception of the first San Francisco Dance Film Festival in the 1970s and Movies by Movers in 2010. Since the inception of Movies by Movers, there has been small, but notable growth among screendance festival curators of color. Some of these festival founders and curators include Robin Gee of the Greensboro Dance Film Festival (2011), Kingsley Irons of Dances Made to Order (with Bryan Koch; 2011), Kat Cole and Eric Garcia of the Tiny Dance Film Festival (2012), Marcus White and Carlos Funn (Funn Foto) of Moving 24 FPS (2015), Donia Salem-Harhoor (with Ann Robideaux) of The Outlet Dance Project, Yea-Jean Choi (with Martheya Nygaard) of kNOwBOX dance (2018), among a growing group of emerging festivals.

Necessarily, this chapter exists for the purpose of describing how I became inspired to utilize ADF's Movies by Movers as a research platform to explore issues of representation from the vantage point of a screendance curator. Weaving philosophical influences that have shaped my understanding of how to look at screendance works with representation in mind and an explanation of my own theoretical foundation that I developed as a result of the research included here, I tell the story of more than five years of inquiry and action that I hope will positively influence the field moving forward.

* * *

As it is a common occurrence to find myself sitting at my desk for hours on end, watching screendance after screendance, I have seen hundreds, if not thousands of films during my time as a screendance curator. I view these pieces through submissions to ADF's Movies by Movers, guest curation engagements, artists who send me their works personally, social media platforms, other festivals and screendance events, and my own searching through archives and special collections. Like many screendance enthusiasts, I am invested in the cultivation and promotion of the genre. To that end, I am interested not only in seeing *what* is being made for the sake of keeping a finger on the creative pulse of the community and for creating a program each year for ADF's Movies by Movers, but I am compelled to question what I see *within* the projects I view to better understand the landscape and trajectory of this art form I wish to serve.

We live in an age where the complexities of identity are being explored and recognized in ways they have never before in human history.[1] In the arts especially, the initiative to create space for varied identities is one that has theoretically been a staple of the arts community, a place where misfits find acceptance, camaraderie, and encouragement. And while the work has been ongoing to make inclusion the norm, there remain disparities and imbalances throughout the artistic landscape that harken back to institutional and societal histories of aesthetic hierarchies and discrimination.

Chapter 9. Investigating Representation as Curatorial Activism

In terms of representation with regard to race, gender, ability, and age in screendance, the landscape boasts shining examples of why the genre has the potential to be such a transcendent platform for featuring bodies not considered apt for the concert stage or a Hollywood movie. However, in considering the demographics found through research conducted within the submission process to ADF's Movies by Movers and other screendance festivals as I will share in Chapter 10, there are areas of disparity that demand examination.

Before presenting my study, I feel the need to pause here to articulate the very specific goals I have in curating a screendance festival.

- First, I wish to articulate and implement a personal curatorial philosophy informed by an understanding of the curatorial landscapes in the fine arts, cinema, live performance, the curatorial lineages of screendance, and my own experiences as a screendance festival founder, curator, researcher, and practitioner. This desire should be evident in the material presented in the chapters leading up to now, and is further encapsulated in the manifesto included at the end of this book.

- Second, I desire to act with the knowledge of how screendance affects audiences with regard to kinetic and emotional empathy, and a recognition that my efforts as a curator have real impact on how patrons understand the arts and choose to support them as a result of their energetic encounters with the work.

- Third, and salient to the conversation in this chapter, I wish to interrogate issues of representation in dance film as an undertaking of curatorial activism. Recognizing that our issues regarding representation are tied to our philosophical and aesthetic forerunners, like concert dance, cinema, and performance art, utilizing the platform of the festival to explore and excavate representational trends has implications for the ways I consider my role in supporting artists and helping to contribute to the well-being of the practice and for the screendance community at large as we continue to evaluate our work and relevance in the world.

It is important to be able to name the impetus for one's interests, associations, and activities in the arts. As a Black woman in screendance, my articulation of these aims is part and parcel of my activism. *Clarity* sets the stage for focused work that leads to productive outcomes and the building of stronger arts communities.

Although I claim many influences in my understanding of screendance and my curatorial practice therein, my curatorial practice with regard to representation is most informed by intersectional feminism. Intersectional feminism—a term which gained popularity beginning in 1989 through the work of critical race theorist Kimberlè Crenshaw—holds that various forms of oppression—racism, sexism, classism—are interconnected and inform the socio-cultural experiences of people whose identities meet at various intersections of oppression. For screendance, this means asking questions about how what we make and program creates space for discourse on the state of the arts at large with regard to aesthetic hierarchies, representation of marginalized communities, and the goals and context of the works that exist in the world. The questions that emerge from being in conversation with the theories of intersectional feminism in looking at and curating screendance compel me to explore what I call *Visual Politics*. In my 2017 article in *The International Journal of Screendance* titled "Visual Politics in American Dance Film: Representation and Disparity," I define the term as such:

> *Visual Politics* is the term I use to consider the vast collection of dance films received through the submission process to ADF's Movies by Movers and the resultant culture, if you will, that highlights the values and ideals inherent in our art form and our community. To further define the term in this context, I consider visual politics to refer to the people and situations we see on screen with respect to the culture created in two-dimensional space by makers and presenters in the collective; influenced by socio-cultural norms in the real world; affected by the lens through which we view the arts and arts industries. Stated simply, on screen are a collection of artifacts that make our values as a community visible [Hagan 2017].

I first began to take notice of disparities in representation on screen in the submission pool to Movies by Movers in 2012. That was the third season of Movies by Movers, and the first year I expanded submissions worldwide, though the majority of submissions came from the United States, as is the case today. As an aside, I want to point out that the highest volume of films that populate screendance festivals across the world come from Western countries. This speaks to the imbalance of representation from non–Western countries across the screendance landscape, generally. The ubiquity of Western imagery means that aesthetic hegemony in screendance exists as a matter of course.

In 2012, I noticed that the majority of the bodies I saw on screen were similar: white, female, relatively young, and consistent in terms of body shape and size. All those who performed on screen were able-bodied (the festival received its first submission featuring visibly disabled performers in 2014). I assumed the demographics I was witnessing were because of a lack of reach in the call for submissions and subsequently assumed that as the festival grew, so would visibly diverse representations found on screen in the submission pool. In 2014, submission numbers to Movies by Movers saw an increase as compared to the years 2010–2013. Still, I felt that the pool was too aesthetically homogenous. As I didn't want to assume that the imbalances I perceived were accurate, I became inspired to embark on a research endeavor that would ultimately yield five years of demographic and aesthetic research (along with retroactive mining of the 2012, 2013, and 2014 seasons) into the submission pool of the Movies by Movers film festival.

In the analysis below, I share methodologies for collecting demographic data on race and gender from the submission pool to ADF's Movies by Movers and the data sets derived from that research. I follow that with explorations of the topics of age and ability as they are experienced in the filmic space. Taken together, these discussions present a platform from which subsequent conversations can flow. In the writing of this book, I realized that there are many topics presented that warrant their own complete text. The topic of representation is one of those, and like many of the discussions in this book, I offer this an invitation to the field for deeper work and am holding myself accountable to continue my own journey.

Why and How—Rationale and Methodology

The demographic data that follows this explanation of methodology consists of several sets of numbers that quantify race and binary gender in the submission pool to ADF's Movies by Movers between the years of 2015 and 2019. In my study, I have chosen to focus most on race and binary gender quantitatively as these two markers of identity are most readily apparent on screen in comparison to gender identities that are a departure from the norm, ability (because of disabilities that would not necessarily be discernable on screen) and age (because unless someone has very clear markers of age, people across a wide span of ages may not actually "look their age"). Gender identity, ability and age have been considered, though, and are looked at qualitatively in this study with regard to how people who identify as queer, trans, disabled or "mature" by the standards of professional dance and mass media are portrayed. Though it is true that people of color and people who identify as non-binary, who are in transition, or are post-transition may not read on screen the way they identify in their everyday lives, this study is about how someone's body reads on screen as compared to dominant aesthetic standards of whiteness and binary notions of gender in American culture. To be clear, the "dominant aesthetic" I reference in this study refers to the historical aesthetic preference for very light skin, bodies read as cisgender, conventional standards of beauty as articulated by the film and television industries, editorial print media and the fashion industry, professional dance, and professional theater which all prioritize youth, as dictated by the white, male gaze, and the ableist culture of the performing arts broadly which has historically rendered disabled people invisible or characters whose presence serves able-bodied narratives.

All of the projects tallied for this study are American in origin, meaning that the artists who made the films are living and working in the United States and their films were made in the United States. Although ADF's Movies by Movers routinely receives submissions from over twenty countries, the largest number of submissions to ADF's Movies by Movers comes from the United States, and the complexities and politics of demographics—most specifically racial politics and gender politics—across the world beg more analysis than the number of films from each individual country outside of the United States represented in the submission pool can accommodate. To carry out the study, I tallied each film in the submission pool, each season individually marking performers, choreographers, and directors in the following categories: white women, women of color, white men, and men of color. I chose to include directors and choreographers in my study because representation behind the camera matters as much as representation on screen, and often, the make-up of production and creative teams gives insight into the politics of what's being seen on screen.

It should be noted that while there are artists who submit more than one film to the festival, no artist has ever submitted enough projects to dramatically tip the scales. Often, each film has a different make-up of people outside of the role that a submitting artist may play. The submitting artist may even shift roles from project to project, making it important to consider each film individually.

To gather data with as much accuracy as possible, I turned to public social media profiles, artist websites, and press about the artists in question. These resources often provided clues as to how the artists self-identify in the world with regard to race and gender identity. Because there are many hundreds of people being accounted for in this study, it was impossible to speak to each of the artists directly. As I thought about the possibility of including a survey for artists as part of their submission materials, I ultimately concluded that while this may have lent more nuance to the study (for example, allowing non-binary, mixed race, and other identities artists may claim to identify as such), artists self-selecting to do the survey would mean three things: that given statistics for survey response generally, the number of overall respondents most likely would not yield a large enough number of data points to do the study on the scale I wished to[2]; that those artists less concerned with or opposed to research on representation in screendance would actively overlook the survey; and finally, that those who have historically been made unsafe through the use of such surveys would be made to feel torn between contributing to the project and attending to their own well-being. As I write this, I recognize how our lives, lived in digital space, complicate our relationships to self-declaration, privacy, and self-promotion as artists. Because of this, I honor all that has been put in plain sight for the world to see, but also those pieces of ourselves that have been necessarily hidden through great effort.

Before presenting the data, I want to stress that the impetus behind collecting numerical data is not to villainize the screendance community as some have assumed.[3] Instead, the point in collecting data from the submission pool to ADF's Movies by Movers and other festivals is to get a more accurate picture of what is being made and submitted to screendance festivals as a whole. This work helps to paint a more vivid picture of the screendance festival circuit and to more clearly tell the stories of individual screendance festivals as we continue to explore the intricacies of the landscape. What do the data sets I've collected say about the politics of soliciting work through submissions to a screendance festival? What does the data say about my ability as a festival director to attract diverse artists to submit to the festival? How can the screendance community use the quantitative and qualitative information included in this chapter and the two following to dream of and create a more equitable festival experience from submission to presentation? What does the screendance community stand to gain from confronting areas of representational disparity? In presenting this study I wish to spur conversation and inspire action among those who curate and present screendance.

Issues of Race in Screendance at ADF's Movies by Movers

In 2018, Miguel Gutierrez wrote an article titled "Does Abstraction Belong to White People?" The piece presents a litany of experiences and questions that invite us to think about the politics of race and representation as they relate to the world of contemporary dance and art. In the article, Gutierrez problematizes the assumed normalcy of dominant aesthetic perspectives and the ubiquity of the white body and the white experience in the arts, as he names the ways non–white artists are expected to navigate the marginalization perpetuated by that ubiquity in order to remain active in the arts communities that may offer space for their work. In particular, he recounts a conversation with a colleague where he questions the persistent lack of artists of color on stage in the downtown dance scene in New York City:

> "Well, that's just who's in the community," she answers, unquestioningly, as if the white choreographers' casting choices have nothing to do with subjectivity or representational politics. That somehow their bodies can be signifiers for a universal experience that doesn't need to look at whiteness as an active choice or as the default mechanism of a lazy, non-existent critique [Gutierrez 2018].

A similar argument is made about the world of cinema by film scholar Maryanne Erigha in her book *The Hollywood Jim Crow: The Racial Politics of the Movie Industry*. She says:

> Hollywood insiders perceive movies as racial entities. Movies with predominantly Black, Latino/a, or Asian casts or lead actors are thought of in terms of their racial makeup, while movies with predominantly white stars are marked invisible. In this way, whiteness is seen as normal and general—just the way movies are... [Erigha 2019, 56].

I think about these quotes in the time of Covid where we meet each other in digital space again and again. In panel discussions, presentations, and in informal meetings, it is clear that the community of screendance skews white and female. I am often the only, or one of a small handful of, people of color in these spaces.

I reference these quotes, and my own experience, because of the relationship of screendance to post-modern dance, performance art, and cinema. In all of these arenas, a general liberality is assumed and seems apparent on the surface. However with a deeper look, we can see that in these spaces segregation, supremacy and discrimination are abundant both historically and contemporarily. It isn't a far reach then to identify the ways dance film may reinforce the same ideals Gutierrez and Erigha name in their work, abstraction being one privilege automatically given to white practitioners in the field as their identity renders them neutral in creative spaces where people of color must always contend with the politics of being non-white and therefore read as non-neutral. This is echoed not only in the numbers of bodies of color found on screen and behind the camera in

128

submissions to ADF's Movies by Movers, but also in the ways that bodies of color are often seen on screen, which I'll delve into more deeply after presenting the data.

In the screendance community specifically, there has only recently been momentum in more widely recognizing disparities in screendance with regard to race as demonstrated by the 2018 issue of the *International Journal of Screendance,* guest edited by Melissa Blanco Borelli and Raquel Monroe, titled "Screening the Skin: Issues of Race and Nation in Screendance." Articles and provocations in this volume open a host of conversations about race that until this issue had never been expressed in what is considered the premiere journalistic resource being published about screendance in the United States. Until this volume, issues of race had only been taken up in a small handful of articles in past volumes, including Melissa Blanco Borelli's 2012 article, "Dancing in Music Videos, or How I Learned to Dance Like Janet... Miss Jackson," and my own 2017 article, "Visual Politics in American Dance Film: Representation and Disparity." From a popular standpoint, we can look to the #oscarssowhite controversy of 2016 (which continued to be a point of conversation through 2019), the debates over blackface and yellowface in the ballet world in 2018 and 2019, controversies over white actors playing characters of color in films recently released in Hollywood, and all the "firsts" of late in the industry, including the appointment of Spike Lee as the head of the 2020 Cannes Film Festival jury—the first African American person to be so appointed—to show that Western society is becoming more aware of the ways whiteness is upheld as a default, even if there is still much more work to be done.

Within submissions sent to Movies by Movers between the years 2015 and 2019, performers of color are seen far less often than white performers on screen. In fact, roughly two-thirds of all the performing bodies featured in American submissions to ADF's Movies by Movers between 2015 and 2019 are white. The percentages for this category are *so* consistent that there is only a 2 percent variance across all ADF's Movies by Movers seasons accounted for in this book. Numbers of performers of color rose steadily in alignment with rising submission numbers between 2012—when the number of white performers versus performers of color was found to be above 80 percent—and 2014. Although this increase was initially encouraging, the stagnation evident in the numbers of bodies of color seen on screen in the submission pools between 2015 and 2019 is ultimately discouraging and says something about who is choosing to submit their work to ADF's Movies by Movers, and who has not yet been invited or feels compelled to participate in the process of getting their work screened at this particular event. Curatorially, that means that screening options featuring bodies of color continue to be more limited than selections featuring white bodies, and that directly impacts how many bodies of color actually make it to the screen each year to be seen by the public.

Men of color are consistently the least represented performers in projects submitted to ADF's Movies by Movers. Looking at the graphs below, one might notice that there was a spike in the number of men of color represented on screen between 2017 and 2018 as compared to 2016. In all instances where a spike in representation of a marginalized group is present in the submission pool, it can be attributed to films (usually one, or a very small handful) that feature a large number of people from that specific demographic, not an even distribution of people across projects. It should be noted that in 2018, the submission process saw one film that credited just over one hundred people of color in it. This film sent the number of men of color over the number of white men for the second time in my study (the first time, the differential was only 1 percent), but ultimately did little to create more parity across the pool. Graph 9.1 represents the years 2015 through 2019 with regard to race. Graph 9.2 represents the numbers for 2018, leaving out the one film that credited over one hundred people of color in the film, to show how the numbers of people of color on screen are not distributed evenly across the pool. This anomaly is examined further in the chapter of case studies comparing demographic data with The Outlet Dance Project and the Mobile Dance Film Festival as there were similar occurrences in their submissions.

In 2019, the UCLA Ralph J. Bunche Center for African American Studies published their annual report on the entertainment industry, *Hollywood Diversity Report: Old Story, New Beginning.* The report notes that minorities seen on screen in leading roles in wide-release films are consistently underrepresented and have been since the first report was published in 2014. The report states:

> Whites remained overrepresented among all top film roles in 2017, claiming 77 percent of the roles (slightly down from 78.1 percent in 2016), while constituting just 60.4 percent of the U.S. population. All other groups remained underrepresented…[Hunt et al., 2019].

This means that although the numbers of white performers are slightly better by comparison in the submissions to ADF's Movies by Movers to those found on Hollywood screens, white performers have always been overrepresented as compared to performers of color with regard to the U.S. population. The report also pointed out discrepancies behind the camera

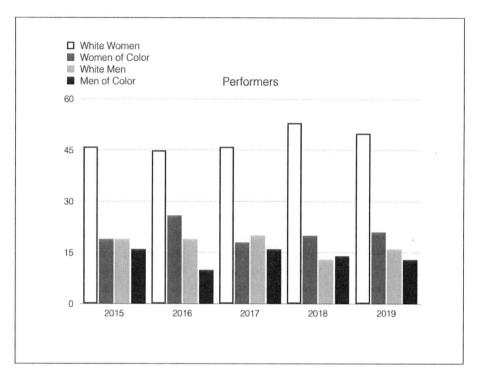

Graph 9.1. Performers 2015–2019

(Hunt et al., 2019). In 2017 just 12.6 percent of Hollywood directors were people of color. The report states, "Minorities would have to multiply their 2017 share by more than three to reach proportionate representation among film directors" (Hunt et al., 2019). Between the 2015 and 2019 seasons of ADF's Movies by Movers, directors of color routinely make up no more than one-quarter of all directors represented. While this may be high as compared to the film industry, screendance is a long way from having a directorial landscape representative of the growing minority in the United States.[4] Men of color are also the least represented in this group. Graph 9.3 demonstrates this trend.

Regarding numbers of choreographers, the data looks strikingly similar. This is represented in Graph 9.4.

Despite efforts to bolster racial diversity among submissions to ADF's Movies by Movers through sharing the call for projects across platforms, articulating a desire for pieces featuring and created by people of color in the call for projects, and the soliciting of such pieces through personal

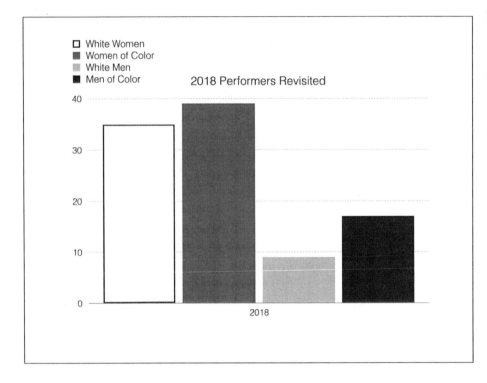

Graph 9.2. Performers Revisited, 2018

invitation, it is evident that there exist barriers to having a more racially diverse submission pool that go beyond an assumption or a perceived reality that works featuring and created by people of color simply don't exist. And while it may be difficult to say why exactly pieces are not making their way to ADF's Movies by Movers, and presumably to other festivals, there are some factors that impact the ability of artists of color in the pursuit of disseminating their work more widely than white artists. Among these factors are access to artistic resources in communities that are under-resourced such as those with low or inadequate employment, and those with schools that cannot support arts programs. Such communities are disproportionately communities of color. Tied to these factors are issues of personal resource which disproportionately affect artists of color in being able to make work and submit their films to multiple festivals that have submission fees. Finally, there is the perception for many artists of color that a lot of the festivals and spaces that host festival activities are not spaces for them. Indie cinema theaters, museums, college campuses—these

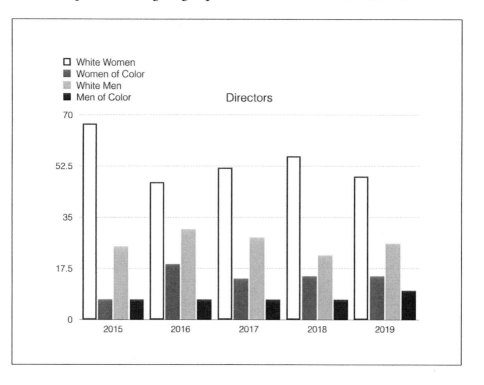

Graph 9.3. Directors 2015–2019

are all spaces with long histories of segregation. The residue of those histories is still felt today through physical structure (many historic movie theaters still have the "colored only" section of their buildings intact, often referred to as "nigger heaven" in the film industry of the early and mid–1900s), location (universities and museums especially are often situated in high-resource and gentrified neighborhoods), the pools of artists routinely presented in these spaces that remain largely homogenous, through the works and scholarship upheld and enshrined in these institutions—which often do not include representation of marginalized groups as part of their accepted canons—and the reticence on the part of many institutions to relinquish their dependence on supremacy as a function of their existence.[5]

Beyond the mere presence of bodies of color on screen and behind the camera, race is closely tied to content when bodies of color do appear. In his 2018 article in the *International Journal of Screendance*, artist and curator Marcus White posits that media in U.S. culture often "spectacularizes black and brown bodies" and goes on to state that the "mediated

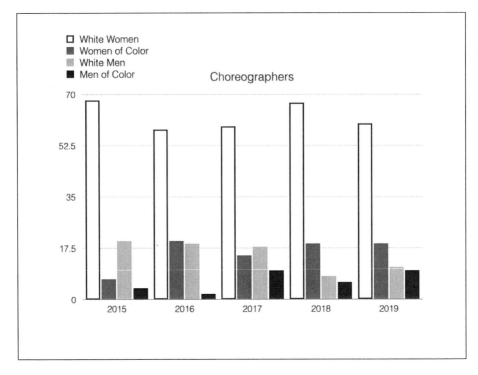

Graph 9.4. Choreographers 2015–2019

narratives of these bodies through film, television, and social media [create] a flood of viscerally irresponsible image-making rooted in stereotypes of quasi-minstrel presentation interlaced with trauma, grief, and death of the black and brown body." This trend has been identified in mainstream cinema and again most saliently through the work of Maryann Erigha:

> The use of race as grounds for difference has implications for employment opportunities and outcomes for members of different racial groups. For U.S. racial and ethnic minorities, invoking race decisions about who should get work and in what capacity leads to marginalization, ghettoization, and stigmatization. Movies with racial minorities attached are devalued and deemed inferior cultural products, which has implications for which roles racial minorities occupy and how their careers progress or are hindered in Hollywood [Erigha 2019].

As screendance created in the United States is often created in the context of American culture, it often cannot separate itself from the influence of segregated histories and dominant narratives. For example, in both 2017 and 2018, there were only eleven American projects with all-Black casts, and of those projects, both years, seven of the eleven were overtly about oppression of some kind. Whether or not those projects were directed by directors of color or not seemed not to influence subject matter, as the subjects themselves are pigeonholed across the pool to display their own oppression. None of the films that featured all-Black casts in 2017 and 2018 were comedies or fantasies. One was quite abstract, but the majority were narrative. It would appear that whiteness allows makers to delve into areas of creativity that are not afforded many artists of color. One can create a film about, for example, a funny sickness, an imaginary friend, food, fairy tales, myths, paganism, unrequited love, house parties, hypnosis, magic doorways, and of course, abstract movement.

It is interesting to note that often bodies of color are being seen through the lens of a white director. Of the eleven projects with all-Black casts in 2017 and 2018, just four and six of those eleven were directed by people of color, respectively. Again, Erigha weighs in with her research into Hollywood about the politics of power dynamics:

> In a 2014 study of the one hundred top-grossing movies of the year, Stacy Smith and colleagues found that when no Black director was behind the camera, less than 11 percent of characters on screen were Black; however, when a Black director was behind the camera, 46 percent of characters on screen were Black. The presence of a Black director increased the number of Black actors more than four times over [Erigha 2019, 33].

So while in this handful of films, there exist white directors directing people of color and their stories, across the screendance landscape, all-white or mostly-white casts are the result of having mostly white directors. Where there may exist eleven all-Black cast films in a submission season, there exist roughly five times that amount of films that feature all-white casts, the vast majority of which also feature all-white creative and production teams.

Going further into subtext (anecdotally), one sees descriptions of these bodies in synopses of the films and, for Black men especially, the words used to describe the bodies on screen are often far different than those used to describe white bodies. Where words that describe a perceived otherness like "powerful" and "mysterious" are used when referencing bodies of color, words that speak to the universal relatability of white bodies are seen in contrast. For example, words like "beauty," "universal," and "human" (used to describe things like "human nature," "human experience," "humanity") speak to the assumed normalcy and further, the assumed humanity of white artists and their products.

There are many reasons for the representational disparities and the differences in conceptual breadth seen on screen between white and non-white bodies. One reason is the history of economics tied to projects created by people of color which shows that the financial risk of putting bodies of color on screen in the film industry has often meant that subject matter is limited to what might be most appealing to white audiences (Erigha 2019). Historically, less money is spent on films with casts and creative teams of color as well. This has often had implications for production value, distribution, and visibility. Although independent filmmakers are not beholden to the financial desires of studios to get their work made, similar histories are at work where arts councils and other institutional funders are concerned. It is often implied, if not unequivocally articulated, that in order to be successful at receiving grants, fellowships, and residencies, that marginalized people must somehow center or situate their marginalization in a way that benefits funding organizations in being seen as supporting diverse voices making "diverse" work (Rosenblatt 2017).

Despite all the challenges outlined here, there are pieces that stand out and buck the status quo. Juel D. Lane's *The Maestro* (2018) takes its inspiration from an Ernie Barnes painting of the same name. Barnes, one of the most famous Black visual artists of the 20th century, was known for his exaggerated, elongated interpretations of the human body in motion and the engaging energy of his pieces. Often, his paintings featured social settings, sporting events, and dance. In the film, Lane harnesses the essence of the original painting that features a lone figure, arms raised as if to begin conducting an orchestra. Lane allows the power of music to overcome him in a duet between himself and a lone radio in an empty room, filling the space with rhythm and undiluted exuberance.

Efeya Sampson's *The Road to Ose Tura (A Prayer Ain't a Prayer Unless You Say It Out Loud)* (2019) invites viewers into the sacred space of a danced prayer. In the film, Sampson chants, sings, sways, and bows repeatedly as she "petitions benevolent forces for blessings." Her body is covered in iridescent droplets of paint and sparkle. She resembles the night sky.

These two films remind us that magic exists everywhere and that the Black body is as full of it as any other body.

The experience of mining data from the submission pool to ADF's Movies by Movers with regard to race has illuminated for me the need to continue digging into these issues. To my knowledge, I am the only researcher on the screendance festival circuit who has taken up the task of exploring the landscape of submissions in this way. Anecdotally, I've even

Juel D. Lane in *The Maestro* (2018). Courtesy Juel D. Lane.

been met with pushback by some in the screendance community who feel that screendance need not concern itself with such undertakings as it distracts from the ideological underpinnings of the practice. To me, this signals discomfort on the part of some in the screendance community and raises questions for me moving forward:

- Should screendance become more representative of our population in the United States, what would change about the genre?
- Could better racial representation in dance film help the arts community as a whole be more open to variations in the types of bodies that are considered pleasing or compelling to watch?
- How can dance film disrupt the notion that young, white, female bodies are the most desirable bodies in dance film?
- How can we set ourselves apart from the mainstream, not just in our conceptual explorations, but in how we present these explorations, with regard to who carries them out?

Unsurprisingly, in 2020 increasing numbers of the films received through the submission process address issues of identity politics, social justice, cultural heritage, and a questioning of what experimentation looks like across those contexts. I believe this trend will continue for seasons to come, as we grapple with the socio-political ethos of our time and continue to see the desire of more marginalized groups vie for their right to be seen and heard.

Gender in Screendance—Where Women Are Concerned

In 2015, I explored what it means to be a feminist in the 21st century and what it means to make feminist art in the context of dance film. In that research I stated:

> For many women and feminist allies, dance film has created a space apart from mainstream media and the traditions of professional dance to practice principles of feminism, including rectifying the presentation of the female body, confronting issues of race, class, and cultural identity, while making room for the kind of creative, intentional activism that has continued to characterize third-wave feminism [Hagan 2016].

With consistently over two-thirds of all the bodies seen in American dance film belonging to women, one might consider the work we have to do, done on that front. After all, women are still fighting for greater representation in positions of leadership in dance companies, in major art exhibitions, and in broadcast and Hollywood.[6]

In some respects, we are doing wonderfully. Pieces like Anabella Lenzu's 2018 *No More Beautiful Dances*—a short piece that explores the complexities of a changing body (i.e., Lenzu represents a body politic outside of the norm in concert dance as a full-figured woman), the experience of giving birth, and immigration all at once in both Spanish and English— show us that screendance supports women in our pursuit of being represented in ways that are real and important to us. Celia Rowlson-Hall's 2015 feature film *MA* gives us a feminist reimagining of the story of the Virgin Mary. Here, the hero's journey, often attributed to male characters in film, is given to a woman whose character is much more nuanced than the virgin-mother-spiritual-vessel figure of the Virgin Mary of biblical rendering. Difficult topics like rape, the complexities of romantic relationships, and sexuality are explored in the film, making the main character's experience relevant to women and female-identified audience members who may share some of those experiences. Too, there is Katherine Helen Fisher's 2019 short, *Revel in Your Body,* featuring dancers Alice Sheppard and Laurel Lawson of the group Kinetic Light. In this slow-motion piece, the dancers soar and flip through the air in their wheelchairs. They create spirals around each other and interact with the structures around them in the parking deck they dance in. The film invites the viewer to revel in the "joy of flight." *Revel in Your Body* pushes the boundaries of how we consider virtuosity to be deployed on screen. Holly Wilder's *The Field* (2018)

138

On a parking rooftop, Alice Sheppard and Laurel Lawson catch each other's forearms in a wheelchair tilt and spin. Alice is a light-skinned multiracial Black woman with curly purple hair, and Laurel is a pale white woman with very short teal hair. Their metallic jumpsuits and metal wheelchairs sparkle in the Atlanta sunshine. Photo by Jared Serfozo.

features a central female character who mitigates negative self-talk, social expectations and societal conditioning by cutting ropes braided into her hair held by actors representing her troubles. The examples are innumerable.

However, the work to fully reconcile the role of women in screen-dance is not yet finished. With consistently half of all the bodies seen on screen belonging to white women exclusively (as seen in the graphs quantifying performers in the previous section on race in screendance), red flags begin to appear within the data. When we dig a little deeper still and consider qualitatively how women appear on screen, there is still concern over the portrayal of the female body on screen as seen through the lenses of conventional notions of aesthetics and the male gaze. Take for example, the presence of nudity in screendance. Beyond obvious biases toward the "dancer body" aesthetic and the desire on the part of performers and directors to present conventionally beautiful people on screen, nudity represents a condition of visibility charged with both stigma and expectation. This condition is employed often enough in screendance that ADF's Movies by

Movers receives a small handful of films each season that feature either partial or full nudity.

Historically, the unclothed female form in Western art has functioned as an object of male desire while also functioning as a site of shame (Berger 1972). Take for example, medieval depictions in paintings of Adam and Eve after eating the apple in the Garden of Eden. While both parties are depicted as naked, often attempting to cover themselves with flora or their hands, Eve must cover more of her body to be considered modest. In Renaissance paintings, naked women are often depicted in repose, passive participants in the observation of their bodies. Their portrayals represent the male interpretation of the ideal woman. Women dancing in such paintings is rare, as movement was seen as an overt sexual expression that put the power of that expression into the hands of the woman instead of the male spectator (Berger 1972). By the early 20th century, the portrayal of the ideal, submissive woman persists as artistic forms such as Broadway and cinema reinforce these notions. Nudity remains a site of both desire and shame, even in experimental circles. If any artist's work is an indication of the tensions created by exhibiting the naked body, it would be Carolee Schneemann. Performance art pieces conceived and executed by Schneemann like *Interior Scroll* (1975), where the artist read aloud a scroll pulled from her vagina, prompted debates about whether the work was in fact a reclamation of female agency or lewd exhibition. It is necessary to point out that while Schneemann's performances may have attracted criticism by some, no women of color in the West have had the freedom to perform such works without much more harsh scrutiny and policing of the body. If there is any indication of this, the 2019 Super Bowl—decidedly *not* an experimental performance art piece—featuring J-Lo and Shakira caused outcries among white America for being too overtly sexualized in the dancing and costume. Though the main performers and dancers showed no more skin than one would find on a family-friendly beach and the dances they performed were the kind you would find commonly at social gatherings, the offense of being women of color in motion was undeniable in the social media posts, articles, and formal complaints to the FCC that followed (CNN, 2020).

In the 2016 submission season, ADF's Movies by Movers received a group of films featuring nudity larger than any other season. In the films one finds conceptual presentations of the body including playfulness, vulnerability, and the-body-as-landscape. As well, there are some instances of nudity that beg the question of whether they are integral to the momentum of the pieces in which they appear or mere decoration. Among the nine films from around the world that featured nudity, six of the projects were directed by women, while three were directed by men. Among the eighteen nude female performers featured in the films (there were two nude male performers tallied as well), only two were identifiably mature women. The rest could be categorized as "young" or "young-looking (no gray hair, no visible wrinkles, athletic bodies)." Of the twenty nude performers tallied among the projects, only two were people of color (women)—one Asian and one Latina. None of the performers are Black. None of the performers are disabled. None of the performers are fat. None of the performers are transgender. None of the directors are people of color. So while the qualitative depictions of many of these nude actors may be in keeping with some of the aims of screendance to create space to reclaim and rethink patriarchal gaze and nudity, it is clear that there is still much attachment to dominant aesthetics. To date, there have been no dark-skinned Black or dark-skinned women of other ethnicities featured in full nudity in the submission pool to ADF's Movies by Movers. There have been no disabled people featured in full nudity. There have been no fat people featured in full nudity. There have been no transgender individuals featured in full nudity. If the goal of showing nudity in screendance is to impart something of the vulnerability and beauty in being naked, then the outcomes of the submissions pool indicates that this is only true for some individuals.

Over the five years concerned with the data in this book—which constitutes over 1,000 films from around the world—nudity is deployed in much the same way in the other festivals explored for the case studies presented in Chapter 10. Again, the vast majority of nude bodies seen on screen are young-looking, thin, and white or very light-skinned. Again, there is an absence of dark skin, fatness, disability, and transness. And while there are histories to contend with in the exhibition of marginalized bodies in the nude where the exhibition of such bodies may become problematic, wouldn't screendance theoretically be a place to mitigate these histories, or at least make commentary? Is it simply a matter of people from marginalized communities not choosing to be featured in the nude, or is there a combination of choice and systematic erasure of marginalized bodies as subjects deemed beautiful enough to show unclothed? Are there elements of the consideration of comfort for the very homogeneous audiences screendance caters to?

To add another layer to this conversation, it becomes clear that women do not often have the luxury of appearing in ways that may undermine one's beauty, even if it is because of something common to the female experience. Take pregnancy, for example. In 2019, ADF's Movies by Movers received a response to a call for works by marginalized directors and choreographers from Ori Lenkinski and Rachel Erdos with their 2018 film, *Carriage*. Featuring seven dancers at various stages of pregnancy, holding and dancing with objects like water balloons, apples, laundry, seeds, and a pile of sticks, the women reflect on the experience of carrying new life and the reorganization that occurs inside a woman's body to make this possible. In reflecting on the film, Lenkinsky states that "pregnant women are nearly invisible in the dance world, on and off stage." She goes on to mention that in our society, women are often encouraged to diminish their role as mothers. In response, this film was created with a team of pregnant women to "give the stage to pregnant women."

As I reflect on the film, on the frequency with which I see depictions of pregnant women in screendance, and on my own experience as a pregnant woman in society, I tend to agree with the directors of the film. Though I can't say that ADF's Movies by Movers has received *no* films featuring pregnant women (2020's lineup actually featured four films that featured or made reference to pregnancy), they are not as common as other depictions of women, and they are almost always *about* the experience of pregnancy.

In dance and in society more broadly, many women feel self-conscious about their bodies during pregnancy because they may be deemed "fat" or otherwise "unattractive." There is also the experience of having one's pregnant body suddenly become the property of others as they touch and inquire about your body and experience uninvited. These experiences may play into why we do not see more pregnant women dancing in screendance without thematic reference to pregnancy.

In sum, the persistence of the white, male gaze in society and in the arts remains a formidable influence in the way we see and choose to display women's bodies and tell their stories. Screendance has the capacity to disrupt this influence through awareness-raising and continued efforts in other directions.

Gender in Screendance—Where Men Are Concerned

Another area of concern in screendance with regard to gender inclusion is the presence of men on screen. Histories of male silencing in dance through societal conditioning and structural repression which stifles men's creative longings in favor of a constructed masculine persona (Hagan 2016) continue to affect male participation in almost anything dance-related in Western culture. Although we have seen some progress in male representation in dance—through incidents like the #boysdance-too movement sparked by a comment made by *Good Morning America* host Lara Spencer about the young Prince George taking ballet in 2019—gender norms persist in screendance, in dance-centric media like *World of Dance* and *Baby Ballroom*, and non–dance-related media where men and women move in societally prescribed gendered vocabularies.

Between the years of 2015 and 2019, the number of men seen on screen among American submissions to ADF's Movies by Movers has never risen above 36 percent. To better put these numbers into perspective, the number of men and women in the United States skews toward a more equal distribution of the sexes. According to the U.S. census, women account for about 51 percent of the population while men account for about 49 percent. What would screendance look like if the numbers of men and women seen on screen across projects were more representative of the American population as a whole? Would we see more varied expressions of gender? In pondering these questions, we must also recognize that it is not only in front of the camera where we see this imbalance in dance film, it exists behind the camera, too. I admit, this is tricky territory as men continue to dominate space in leadership roles in dance companies, in directorial positions in Hollywood, and in other positions of leadership in the arts. Screendance has offered women a place to take up leadership where other avenues have been much less accessible. However, when the balance between the sexes is skewed largely in any direction, it is hardly cause for celebration if it is (a) because of a social stigma, and (b) shows sharp disparities where men of color are concerned, reinforcing histories of the erasure of men of color in such positions. White, female choreographers consistently account for over half of all choreographers represented in any given season of ADF's Movies by Movers submissions, while male choreographers have accounted for only about one quarter of all choreographers in the submission pools across all seasons. The picture is similar for directors with male directors representing on average 35 percent of all directors represented in the submission pools for all the seasons. As demonstrated earlier in the graphs above, men of color are the consistently the least represented in these categories.

Gender in Screendance—LGBTQIA+

Because it is harder to ascertain whether or not someone identifies as part of the LGBTQIA+ community by looking at them, and because those who may not consider themselves to be in safe community or do not wish to out themselves as queer or trans may not publicly proclaim their affiliation, I do not tally performers and those in positions of leadership based on whether they identify as part of the LGBTQIA+ community. Yes, the study is done so that no one's identity is explicitly linked to their person as they appear on screen or behind the camera, but things like skin color and gender as perceived through a cisgender lens are easy to see much of the time. And even though artists may choose to identify themselves on social media or through other means, it is important to note that there exists a history of data being used against the LGBTQIA+ community where such information has been and still is used as a vehicle for both discrimination and erasure. In fact, the U.S. census came under fire for not accounting for gender identity on its most recent survey. Though the 2020 census *did* account for same-sex couples living under the same roof—a more recent development in the history of the census in recognizing people and families outside of traditional norms—the survey did not have any options to identify oneself as non-binary, trans, or queer which left large swaths of the community feeling silenced.

What does this mean for film, and more specifically, for screendance? Simply put, it means that we have work to do to better represent people from the LGBTQIA+ community and their stories while decentering white, cisgender norms that undermine the diversity with which people experience their identity. Just because there are visible representations of queer and trans individuals dancing on television (think *Pose, Legendary, The Prom)* does not mean that mainstream media is not homophobic and transphobic. Likewise, it does not mean that dance, with its continued dependence on traditional gender roles to continue perpetuating hierarchical structures in dance institutions and to continue to uphold dominant notions of beauty, is not homophobic and transphobic. Examples abound, some of which I have made in my earlier writings on dance and the screen. In the 2017 provocation in the *International Journal of Screendance* I mention earlier, I cited Anthony Bryant being deemed "too feminine" by the panel of judges in his dancing on a *So You Think You Can Dance* audition in 2005. Other, more recent incidents point to this dependence too, such as the reprimand and/or ousting of several men in positions of leadership in dance for their abuse of power through gendered dynamics, and more saliently, the appropriation and performance of queer dance forms without acknowledgment of their origins from Madonna's "Vogue" to the whitewashing of dance forms from queer, BIPOC communities on TikTok (Pearce 2020).

In my frustration at the persistent lack of diversity across the screen-

dance landscape, I made a call for pieces created by marginalized directors and choreographers as part of the 2019 submission period. Instead of
a survey where one checks a series of boxes, artists were invited to respond
to the question of whether one felt that they or their work was marginalized through a narrative statement. Responses ran the gamut from those
citing marginalization as first-time filmmakers, filmmakers creating work
with no budget, filmmakers who have never had their work shown outside of a specific region, to those citing their inclusion in a marginalized
group like BIPOC or queer artists. It is interesting to note that all the projects that claimed to be marginalized because of their status as first-time
filmmakers, because of a lack of funds with which to create their works, or
because of limited visibility outside of their immediate area (which in this
case was a large, metropolitan area) were submitted by white, female artists. Of the projects that featured artists who identified themselves as marginalized, 33 percent claimed to be by artists in the LGBTQIA+ community.
Of those, almost two thirds were in some way thematically about identify-
ing as queer. Like the limitations placed on non-white artists in the kinds of
content they may make and present to the world, it would seem that this is
the case for the queer community as well. This is echoed in that mainstream
shows that feature queer or trans actors almost always include those actors
in or responding to concerns related to the LGBTQIA+ experience.

Even so, those representations of the LGBTQIA+ experience in
screendance are important and the genre has long served as a platform for
those voices to experiment, express, and share. Each season, there are several pieces to be found among the submissions that are affirming representations of the LGBTQIA+ community.

In 2015 for example, there emerged a number of dance films which
highlighted LGBTQIA+ themes. Hence, I had the opportunity to curate
a screening dedicated to exploring those themes. All three of the films
selected for the screening stood out for different reasons. *Notes from There
(Notas Desde Allá)*, made in 2015 and directed by Ann Prim, showed two
women in love across borders—the struggle of the immigration process,
coupled with the power of art to bolster the spirit. *Intrinsic Moral Evil*
by Harm Weistra (2013) is "a tale of identity and coming of age."[7] Featuring three performers seemingly embroiled in a multi-faceted love trian-
gle between two men and a woman, the audience is invited to draw their
own conclusions as the female character reveals themselves to be male. The
standout film of the evening, and the longest film, was *From the Heart of
Brahma*. This documentary features Prumsodun Ok, a queer, Cambodian
dance artist whose mission is to both honor and question the traditions

from which he comes. The film opens discussions about cultural identity, sexuality in art, and the impact society has on young people. In a 2015 interview posted on the now-defunct Movies by Movers website, filmmaker/director Carl Off said of the film:

> The dance itself is seen as one of a few symbols that make up the Cambodian identity—an identity that was nearly lost when 90% of all dancers, artists and intellectuals were killed in the Khmer Rouge auto-genocide between 1975 and 1979. This story is about Cambodia, Cambodian Classical Dance and Prum's mission to make the art form inclusive of all practitioners while sharing it with his immediate community and the world. An element of Prum's work—addressing social justice, particularly LBGTQ concerns—has received both support and controversy in Cambodia, because he is a male dancer practicing a female form and because he introduces same sex love in ancient heteronormative mythologies.

Ok's disruption of gender norms in classical dance is an important step to making dance and dance film places where gender can be fluid, just like dance itself.

Subsequent seasons have included highlights like Leen Michael's 2016 film, *Your Approval Is Not Essential,* which follows two women as they cultivate freedom in a world that wants them to be restrained and predictable. Cesar Brodermann's 2017 film, *Are You Holding Me, or Am I Holding Myself?,* investigates "what it is to create and struggle with certain

Photograph still from the movie *From the Heart of Brahma,* featuring dancer/ choreographer Prumsodun Ok. Courtesy Carl Off.

boundaries that stem from self-reflection/self-torment over past experiences, and the means by which we think we can achieve an ideal emotional or physical state."[8] *Unapologetic Me: BLACK|GAY|MAN,* directed by Justin Dominic (2018), explores the intersectional experience of being Black, male, and gay in contemporary society through luscious movement, personal narration, and original music by Nathan Bajar.

Though the films listed are international in scope, it is heartening to think that these and other films may bolster support and visibility of the LGBTQIA+ community. And while not all the films in the submission pool are as sensitive or aware as others, there seems to be an increasing awareness of LGBTQIA+ artists, as positive representations of such individuals in mass media is making a slow, but noticeable increase as well.

Where Age Is Concerned

Given the numerical explorations with regard to race and gender and the very obvious disparities discussed thus far in this study, where does that leave us with regard to age and ability?

As the vast majority of practitioners in screendance come from professional dance, it is no surprise that ageism is a topic that requires some examination in this work. While dancers are performing later into their lives than previous generations, more mature dancers still face discrimination and the danger of invisibility in comparison to their younger counterparts. It could be argued that much of screendance has the danger of becoming about youthful beauty and virtuosity instead of a nuanced exploration of the mediated body. Dance on screen in more mainstream venues most often features very young dancers, doing almost-impossible feats in front of judges meant to be wowed (the jaw-dropping acrobatics of the young performers on *World of Dance* come to mind). And although screendance has often made the distinction of its aims as different from that of dance on the commercial screen, the age of digital technology and social media is blurring the lines of what belongs in what genre. Many would argue that social media is one of the reasons why we see many more films made in recent years that are more about the "wow" factor and high production value than about making screendance. The need for screendance to function as both art and promotion makes the temptation to create virtuosic videos, especially for emerging artists, hard not to fall into. And as 21st-century society keeps showing us, youth and beauty sell. There have been artists railing against ageism since the advent of film, and we see once more the work of women boiling to the surface at the vanguard of these discussions and creations. Doris Chase, mentioned much earlier in this book, is well-known for her foray into television which included a six-part series titled *By Herself* that tackles the very topic of the aging woman in society. It is one of Chase's most frequently screened collection of works. Although this may have opened the door to other female artists following suit, it remains a struggle to be represented as an older person on screen, especially an older female person.

Like those films described earlier that represent women on screen in affirming ways, there exist many worthy instances where mature dancers are depicted in nuanced circumstances in dance film. *Home Exercises* (2017) by Sarah Friedland shows a community of elders moving through everyday experiences which become choreographies through the mediation of the body through the lens, the editing process, and the collaborative relationship evident between the subjects and the filmmaker. While these performers are clearly not "dancers," the care with which the filmmaker portrays them makes this film stand out. *Meeting Place* (2015) by Amanda Knapp shows two mature dancers, a man and a woman, dancing

Still from Sarah Friedland's *Home Exercises* (2017). Courtesy Sarah Friedland.

together in what feels like a sacred ritual in a clearing in the forest, with full agency. These dancers are clearly seasoned professionals whose artistry comes through the screen through their dancing and the skillful cinematic composition on the part of the filmmaker. Pam Kuntz's *Ellis Won't Be Dancing Today* artfully depicts the experience of a woman and her husband who has Alzheimer's disease as they navigate the medical system and their love of dancing. Though all of these films and more are in their own individual ways diverse representations of the aging body on screen, I'd like to note that in my experience a majority of films featuring older bodies on screen are directed by younger filmmakers. What does it mean when mature performers are seen through the lens of someone who does not share their life experience? Does there exist a stigma around age behind the camera, too? If so, why? What can the screendance community do to better support aging performers and filmmakers? These questions and others inform my understanding of the presence of varied abilities on screen and behind the camera, too.

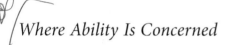

Where Ability Is Concerned

You may remember that one of my very first experiences creating screendance was in collaboration with a group of artists with various disabilities at The Enrichment Center of Winston-Salem creating what would become the short film, *Breathe In, Breathe Out*. That project opened my eyes to a multitude of experiences and concerns that I had up until that point not considered deeply. First, my immediate understanding that much of my formal training in dance was far from inclusive. It was in fact, quite exclusive and notions of "ability" were more related to a set of narrow guidelines dictated by an ableist culture in the movement arts than the breadth of aesthetic ideas, possibilities, and ways of being that exist in the world. Second, the potential of cinema, and more specifically, screendance, is a space where one can both subvert and reimagine those guidelines that dictate aesthetic value in the concert dance and mainstream cinema worlds that I was previously accustomed to. Third, as an able-bodied person with limited knowledge about the disability community at the time, my role as a solo director and producer of the piece ultimately reinforced ableist narratives. I am quite certain that the piece we created did not display those understandings as clearly as other works I'll reference in this discussion, but the simultaneous challenge and boon of learning to communicate with each and every participant, and have each of their creative voices represented in the piece as co-choreographers helped to develop my awareness of the politics of creative agency and representation with regard to people whose abilities fall outside of what dominant culture considers to be the norm, and frankly, forced me to check myself and do better.

While I have not had another chance since the making of *Breathe In, Breathe Out* to create another screendance work with an inter-ability or fully-disabled group of artists, my constant watching of screendance has continued to shape my awareness of when and how artists of different abilities are represented across the landscape of screendance. The first few seasons of Movies by Movers, we did not receive any films featuring performers with visible disabilities through the submissions process. I am certain, however, that performers with invisible disabilities are far more common than we may think, even if their physicality fits within accepted aesthetic norms. Since 2014, the number of films submitted that feature performers of various abilities has risen steadily, much like films with performers of color. Ultimately though, they remain underrepresented in the submission pool for each year Movies by Movers has received films featuring disabled performers. According to the 2019 Annual Report on People with Disabilities in America, the percentage of the population that identifies as having disabilities is around 13 percent (Institute on Disability, 2020). The percentage of films submitted to Movies by Movers that feature performers with visible disabilities has never approached 13 percent and hovers at about 4 percent world-wide in any given season. Even so, many of the films that have come through the submission process, and those that have been solicited for screening through active searching, demonstrate the ways self-identified disabled artists and their able-bodied collaborators are challenging the status quo and redefining what artistic agency means in screendance.

Although there are many examples of how disabled performers are showing up in ways that negate the idea that disability means a deficit of some sort, there are quite a few thoughts in my mind that come to the surface as I continue to contemplate issues of representation and disability in screendance. One is that there are dance films I have seen that do the opposite of redefining sufficiency and deficit where ability is concerned and teeter on the edge of patronizing. The role of the savior-director, someone who puts people on display as if to say, "Look at what these performers can do, *despite* their disabilities!" is one that remains visible on the festival circuit and can be an easy role to fall into if one is not conscientious. I will not name any specific pieces where I have felt this is the case as I do not wish to disparage anyone's efforts. Many of the pieces that have come across my desk are ones I am certain were created with the utmost care in their intentions, but how do we keep our implicit biases in check, especially where obvious power dynamics are involved, for instance, when adult filmmakers and choreographers are working with young performers? Or when directors and choreographers who fall within the norm of cognitive ability are working with artists who are neurodivergent? It is worth mentioning that like *Breathe In, Breathe Out*, a large number of the films that are received through the submission process do not include disabled people in directorial positions. Worth mentioning as well are the few publications and formal discussions on disability in screendance that exist in the available scholarship. However, one such article can be found in the *International Journal of Screendance*. Written by Sarah Whatley in 2010, "The Spectacle of Difference: Dance and Disability on Screen" problematizes the assumption that the viewership of works that include disabled performers are themselves able-bodied, and the hierarchies at play that often pigeonhole disabled artists into performing their disabilities as part and parcel of the work. In the article she writes:

> depending on the bodily mode of engagement of the viewer, this identification might reinforce a notion of human difference, thereby allowing the viewer to "witness spectacles of bodily difference without fear of recrimination by the object of this gaze" (Mitchell and Snyder 157). Dancers with disabilities therefore have good reason to feel anxious about how their work is seen and evaluated in its own terms, prompting them to foreground their own experience of disability and their marginalization within an art form that has traditionally fixed the gaze on the sleek, perfect, flawless dancing body and which too often conforms to conventional notions of beauty [Whatley 2010].

Within disability communities as they relate to dance performance and screendance, there exist hierarchies as well. In some films, like Pelle Hybbinette's *Wrecked Pulse* (2018), featuring dancers Peder Nilsson and Madeleine Månsson from the Swedish contemporary dance company, Skånes Dansteater, both able-bodied and disabled dancers are seen moving at a high level of physicality. In the film, Månsson appears seated in a space full of large water pipes. We find Nilsson draped over one of these pipes, and subsequent cuts find both dancers engaged in various short explorations of the space. While we see Månsson briefly in her wheelchair, the first time we see the duo moving together, they are crawling army-style across the expanse of this industrial space. What follows is an intricate *pas-de-deux* between Nilsson (able-bodied) and Månsson in her wheelchair that includes multiple lifts and complex movement patterns. Although this film represents just one manifestation of inter-ability dance, many in the disability community are not physically capable of the kinds of movement seen in this piece and questions like "Who is too disabled to appear in a screendance?" inevitably arise.

Pioneer Winter Collective's 2017 *Gimp Gait* appears as a "solo for two,"[9] where dancer/choreographer Pioneer Winter supports dancer/choreographer Marjorie Burnett through a solo choreography. The opening of the piece is jarringly confrontational, with Burnett and Winter slowly walking (Winter)/rolling (Burnett in her electric wheelchair) into the performance space—a studio full of mirrors all facing inward toward the center of the space—flipping off and cursing at the audience. Winter subsequently supports Burnett physically in a multitude of ways as she flexes and arches her spine, walks across the space, and moves her arms. As the piece progresses, Burnett alludes to public perceptions of disabled bodies and concepts like sexuality and autonomy as she sticks her finger in her mouth, touches various parts of her body, and lets her hair down out of the ponytail she is seen wearing at the beginning of the piece. Through the collaborative nature of the piece, *Gimp Gait* also challenges notions of age in dance and cinema by featuring Burnett, who is in her mid–50s, as the focal performer and Winter, who is in his 20s, in a supporting role.

Among the few films that have come through the submission pool to ADF's Movies by Movers that feature a fully-disabled cast and directorial team is *Waking the Green Sound: a Dance Film for the Trees (2015)*, co-directed and choreographed by members of the performance collective, Wobbly Dance. Its primary members, Yulia Arakelyan and Erik Ferguson, appear on screen with guest artist Grant Miller in a whimsical journey into nature that is equal parts dream and ritual. Over the course of the fifteen-minute film, viewers are made privy to a tea party where the performers engage in a flower-induced colloquy, to the forest where they appear clad in fabric tied about their bodies and white paint on their exposed skin, moving among the leaves on the forest floor, to a shrine where each performer is seen alone, seemingly engaged in an internal, emotional process or catharsis.

As we grapple with the politics of ableist culture as it is seen and experienced on screen, we also have to grapple with the ways screendance festivals are ableist events. For example, so many of the spaces that we hold our events in do not cater to those in wheelchairs. Old theaters and community spaces do not always have accessible entry and exit. In cities where getting around is a difficult task, many festivals do not or are unable to exist in spaces close to accessible subway stations, for example. Those with sensitivities to certain types of sound or light may also find screendance

Marjorie Burnett and Pioneer Winter in *Gimp Gait* (2017). Courtesy Pioneer Winter.

festivals difficult to navigate, if no information exists on how to make screening options accessible to those that need it. Or, what about inviting those people who are visually impaired to attend a screening? We can look to the disability community, and to the disability film festival community, for answers on how to be more inclusive in our event-making. For example, the Superfest in California has narrated screenings so those who cannot see the films well, or at all, can still enjoy the content. ADF's Movies by Movers took a cue from this festival and included narrated screenings in 2020.

As a conclusion to this chapter, I believe this work has positively affected my ability to read screendance more critically. I believe also that my awareness of how people create and experience art in general has been heightened. As a maker, I am more aware now of how my work may be contextualized by audiences and presenters and how that work is both in alignment with and in opposition to the status quo. As an educator and scholar of screendance, I can use this study to engage students and fellow scholars in a multifaceted dialogue about screendance as an art form and as a form of cultural capital. Most importantly, as a curator, I am driven by this journey to become a stronger advocate for marginalized voices. I felt going into the study that I already had a keen awareness of these issues, but I find in hindsight this was simply not true. I feel more equipped to speak with depth and eloquence about the need for the arts and for screendance to have a reckoning that compels more people to embark on similar journeys of consciousness-raising.

As an opening to the possibilities this work offers, I segue to the next chapter, which is a very necessary continuation of this work. In this, I recognize that the end of this work only exists at the end of our curiosity. The choice to keep digging is one that will continue to reveal new and ever-more valuable insights into the worlds made possible through creative pursuits, and to our relationships to those works and their makers, which does not exclude ourselves.

CHAPTER 10

Case Studies

During the years it took to carry out my study, I wondered intensely about other festivals and whether or not their data would look similar or different than my own. Thus, in 2018 I decided to stop simply wondering and began looking for opportunities to create the data sets I dreamed about. Having more data would inevitably give more depth to the work and invite more people to the table for this important conversation on representation in screendance. In embarking on an extension of my study of ADF's Movies by Movers to include other festivals, I had so many questions:

- Is the consistency of representational data found in the submissions to my own festival echoed in the submission pools to other festivals?
- If my data is quite different than any one festival with regard to representation, what might be the underlying causes? If not, what does that mean for the screendance landscape moving forward?
- How will having such information available to the screendance community help strengthen awareness of the ways the well-being of the genre can be better supported?
- Are there changes that need to be made in how young screendance makers are educated, how we consider our own professional work, and how festivals are curated?
- What does the data from a handful of festivals say about the inclusivity of the screendance community?
- What does the data say about screendance's relationship to its various histories, and what long-held hierarchies might screendance be reifying or assuaging?

One challenge to completing the task of gathering data from other festivals is that many of the festivals I approached were not interested in having their submission pools examined. Festival directors and curators worried about how the knowledge of such a study would be seen by would-be submitters. "Would this affect submission numbers?" They wondered. Would this affect how people viewed the ethical compass of the festival? My own opinion on such hesitation was that the study might reveal some truths that may be uncomfortable or undesirable to organizations believing themselves to be inclusive as a matter of course. No one wants to be told that despite their best efforts at attracting diverse artists to their calls for work that they, in fact, are not succeeding. I have experienced firsthand the frustration of facing the reality of my own data. Through my own efforts—my presence as a woman of color, explicit calls for projects by artists from marginalized communities, leniency with waivers for submission fees for artists who express need, and my very public scholarship on the matter—I have not been able to make the impact I have hoped to make through conventional means. Through this experience, I realize that this study is my first step toward making a difference. Thus, in approaching festivals to run data sets on their submissions, the first festival to accept my invitation to participate was The Outlet Dance Project.

Case Study 1—The Outlet Dance Project

Since 2005, The Outlet Dance Project has produced an annual dance festival in Hamilton, New Jersey, at the Grounds for Sculpture, a 42-acre outdoor sculpture park, museum, and arboretum that hosts regular arts programming throughout the year. Hamilton is about sixty miles from New York City, which means that the artists living, working, and passing through the metropolitan area of New York City are accessible and as a result, the area sees much cross-pollination with its more metropolitan neighbor. In addition to clear connections there, the festival also boasts a national and international reach. The screendance portion of The Outlet Dance Project annual festival was added in 2011. The festival's mission statement is as follows:

> The Outlet Dance Project is committed to providing artists who identify or have identified as women an opportunity to share their artistic vision through site-specific dance, film, and work created for the stage. In partnership with Grounds For Sculpture—an internationally renowned contemporary sculpture park—collaboration, community building, and interdisciplinary experimentation are an integral part of the festival. The Outlet is dedicated to supporting all traditional and nontraditional dance forms. The festival celebrates the intersections of visual and moving arts, exploring relationships between sculpture and dance, between place and movement.[1]

Chapter 10. Case Studies

In 2019, demographics from American screendance submissions to the 2018 festival were collected. In keeping with the data collected between 2015 and 2019 for ADF's Movies by Movers, this collection is focused on binary gender and race. All number sets expressed reflect the 2018 season for both festivals. As in the process with submissions to Movies by Movers, all films identified as American submissions (created by artists who identify their work as having American origins/affiliations in their submissions) were counted individually. Like the study of the submissions to ADF's Movies by Movers, each film had the following roles tallied: director(s), choreographers(s), performer(s). The tables below express how the two festivals compare numerically, while the narrative portions of this case study express how the two festivals differ in terms of the artists they reach and how their stated mission impacts how the curatorial process is undertaken.

Directors

White Female Directors	Women of Color Directors	White Male Directors	Male of Color Directors
TODP: 57%	24%	11%	8%
MBM: 56%	15%	22%	7%

Total Women Directors for TODP: 81%   Total White Directors for TODP: 68%
Total Men Directors for TODP: 19%   Total People of Color Directors for
TODP: 32%

Total Women Directors for MBM: 71%   Total White Directors for MBM: 78%
Total Men Directors for MBM: 29%   Total People of Color Directors for MBM:
22%

The percentage of white female directors for both festivals is comparable. It is clear that The Outlet Dance Project attracts more women of color directors than ADF's Movies by Movers. This can be attributed both to The Outlet Dance Project's stated mission of supporting female-identified artists and co-director Salem-Harhoor's relationship to the South Asian dance community which is readily apparent in the submission pool. Female-identified directors of color are still underrepresented in both festivals. The percentage of white male directors in submissions for ADF's Movies by Movers is high in comparison to The Outlet Dance Project as MBM does not have a stated mission of privileging the work of a specific demographic and therefore does not disqualify work that falls outside of stated demographic parameters. In a space more specifically tied to the concert dance world and the histories of the American Dance Festival, the percentage of men overall, and specifically white men, would be higher than that of a space with lesser ties to those formalized, historically hierarchical communities and a charge to represent and support female artists who are underrepresented in the arts landscape broadly. Male directors of color in both festivals are almost equally underrepresented, which is consistent with demographics taken for ADF's Movies by Movers over the last five years.

Choreographers

White Female Choreographers	Women of Color Choreographers	White Male Choreographers	Male of Color Choreographers
TODP: 67%	24%	4%	5%
MBM: 67%	19%	8%	6%

Total Women Choreographers for TODP: 91%

Total Men Choreographers for TODP: 9%

Total Women Choreographers for MBM: 86%

Total Men Choreographers for MBM: 14%

Total White Choreographers for TODP: 71%

Total People of Color Choreographers for TODP: 29%

Total White Choreographers for MBM: 75%

Total People of Color Choreographers for MBM: 25%

The percentage of white female choreographers between the two festivals is comparable. We see to a lesser degree than that of the director category that the percentages of women of color choreographers are in favor of The Outlet Dance Project, but still underrepresented in both festivals. Both festivals show clearly that the largest percentage of choreographers are women overall, with only a 5 percent difference in totals. Similar to the pool of directors, there is a higher percentage of white male choreographers in the submission pool to ADF's Movies by Movers. Male choreographers of color are similarly underrepresented in this category, as is in keeping with numbers for ADF's Movies by Movers over the past five years. It should be noted that The Outlet Dance Project's men of color choreographers outnumber their white counterparts by 1 percent.

Performers

The numbers of performers as they are represented in the table below have remained fairly stable in all the years of collecting demographics for

ADF's Movies by Movers. However, in 2018, the numbers were largely the same save the inclusion of one film that had over 100 credited bodies of color in it. In the submissions to The Outlet Dance Project, there existed a film that featured twenty-one non-credited male performers of color. While these men were not the lead actors in the film, they played a significant role to the extent that the film would not have existed without them and their dancing, even if they were not cast as main subjects. In each instance, these added bodies of color tipped the scales. The exclusion of the names of the performers in the submission to The Outlet Dance Project speaks to a history of erasure of people of color in film. The trend of white bodies in screendance showing up in spaces that are predominantly spaces of color while not acknowledging the ways their presence objectifies the uncredited people of color in those spaces presents fodder for deeper discussion of the politics of how we take up space socio-politically. In the table below. asterisks indicate data that includes the films with large numbers of cast members of color.

White Female Performers	Women of Color Performers	White Male Performers	Male of Color Performers
ODP: 57%	22%	9%	12%
*ODP: 53%	21%	8%	18%
MBM: 53%	20%	13%	14%
*MBM: 35%	39%	9%	17%

Total Women Performers for TODP: 79%

Total Men Performers for TODP: 21%

*Total Women Performers for TODP: 74%

*Total Men Performers for TODP: 26%

Total Women Performers for MBM: 73%

Total Men Performers for MBM: 27%

*Total Women Performers for MBM: 74%

*Total Men Performers for MBM: 26%

Total White Performers for TODP: 66%

Total People of Color Performers for TODP: 34%

*Total White Performers for TODP: 61%

*Total People of Color Performers for TODP: 39%

Total White Performers for MBM: 66%

Total People of Color Performers for MBM: 34%

*Total White Performers for MBM: 44%

*Total People of Color Performers for MBM: 56%

Screendance from Film to Festival

Where the first set of numbers is concerned (without the two films added), there exists only a 4 percent margin for the number of white women performers between ADF's Movies by Movers and The Outlet Dance Project, with a slightly higher number of white female performers going to The Outlet Dance Project. Numbers for women performers in total is over two-thirds of total performers for both festivals, with a slightly higher percentage represented in The Outlet Dance Project's submission pool. This category is the only category where men of color are represented in higher numbers than white men. In the data collected for ADF's Movies by Movers' submissions, this is a relatively new development that has only begun to take place over the final two years of the study. This can be most attributed to films concerning the plight of Black men in the United States specifically, and the rise of films exploring movements like the Movement for Black Lives (M4BL). So, while this is in theory a good thing, these numbers represent a specific creative and aesthetic box that the majority of the men of color participating in these films exist in.

With regard to the numbers collected after considering the two films mentioned above, The Outlet Dance Project experienced a 5 percent difference all around. For ADF's Movies by Movers, this addition was most impactful, creating for the first time in ADF's Movies by Movers' history a higher percentage of people-of-color performers than white performers. The numbers of women and men performers stayed largely skewed toward women.

In sum, it is clear that The Outlet Dance Project upholds its mission to represent and support female-identified artists. Anecdotally, their support of the LGBTQIA+ community is also visible in the submission pool. Even so, there are caveats to who gets to present as and create around recognizably LGBTQIA+ themes. The film most recognizable as an LGBTQIA+ film in the pool was created by a fully white leadership and cast. What is evidently clear in the submission pool is the connections the directors have to their chosen dance communities. The South Asian dance community being quite present in the submissions is a testament to the directors' efforts to highlight these communities and non–Western dance forms. With regard to race specifically, while the percentage of people of color in total is higher than ADF's Movies by Movers—especially where directors are concerned— there remains an issue of colorism where the vast majority of people of color represented both behind and on screen can be described as "Asian," "Hispanic," or "ethnically ambiguous." As stated before, the vast majority of films that represent Black bodies especially are based on themes of oppression as experienced by Black communities. As explained earlier in this

The Outlet Dance Project 2017 Panel at Grounds for Sculpture. Pictured from left to right: Ann Robideaux, Donia Salem Harhoor, Tina Motoki, Wendy Angulo, Kristin Hatleberg, Jade Charon. Photo by Gala Derroisne. Courtesy The Outlet Dance Project.

chapter, this puts Black makers and bodies in conceptual boxes that limit the scope of how people are invited to consider their aesthetic breadth and their ways of existing in the world. This is visible throughout the landscape of screendance and is echoed in the submission pools to ADF's Movies by Movers between 2015 and 2018.

When comparing these two festivals, it is clear that young, white, female bodies remain the most valuable and visible bodies in American screendance. It is clear also that in leadership roles (directors and choreographers), men of color remain at a sharp disadvantage. These conclusions are tied to our collective notions about beauty and aesthetics in Western culture, where "conventionally beautiful" bodies are young, white, and thin. In dance and screendance, this is amplified as the profession asks us to conform to expectations around athleticism, sexual objectification, and what early film and television makers called "agreeable"[2] people to represent us all in mass media. Further, with dance's historical relationship to gender dynamics in the West where men are concerned, it seems that screendance continues to grapple with the question of men participating on a larger scale. Additionally, the field is struggling with undoing historical hierarchies that place men of color lower than white men when it comes to questions of competency in leadership. Where a festival like ADF's Movies by Movers is concerned, where films from large ballet companies and medium to large modern dance companies routinely come in, it makes sense that there would be a higher percentage of white men represented in roles of leadership. This is routinely the case in the dance world, where white men make up the majority of directors and choreographers in the upper realms of the industry.

The Outlet Dance Project provides women-identified and non-binary makers and performers a place to have their work celebrated in a non-traditional, accessible format. The directors are aware and sensitive to the challenges of being women and non-binary in the broader arts landscape. They are committed to their stated mission and, the festival will, for all intents and purposes, remain an important entity on the screendance festival circuit. While these are admirable traits of the festival, given the many similarities between ADF's Movies by Movers' submissions and their own, questions still remain as to how we can shift paradigms of representation across screendance to be more inclusive as a whole.

Case Study 2—Mobile Dance Film Festival

"Smartphones. Sensational Dance." That's what the landing page says on the 92nd Street Y website, where the Mobile Dance Film Festival has taken place each year since 2018. From the explorations in earlier chapters of this book, you already know the ways in which the Mobile Dance Film Festival is an outlier compared to other screendance festivals in existence at the time of the writing of this book. Most saliently, the Mobile Dance Film Festival's requirement that the work be made with smartphones and the accessibility that comes with a mandate to use consumer equipment means that the submission pool to the festival will be, by definition, vastly different than that of festivals with a more traditional approach to filmmaking desired. While there existed some overlaps in pieces submitted to ADF's Movies by Movers in 2018 with those submitted to The Outlet Dance Project that same year, there was not a single film overlap in the 2019 submission pool to the Mobile Dance Film Festival and the 2019 season submissions to ADF's Movies by Movers. This is the main reason I wanted to analyze the submission pool of the Mobile Dance Film Festival.

I approached this analysis with the following questions:

- Does easier access to equipment for more filmmakers and a free submission application mean that the submission pool to the festival will be more diverse than the submission pools to ADF's Movies by Movers and The Outlet Dance Project?
- Does the informalization of filmmaking through the use of smartphones mean that more "non-dancers" or non-professional dancers will submit works for consideration?
- Does the assumed ubiquity of smartphones across many regions of the world mean that greater diversity of style will be observable in the submissions to the Mobile Dance Film Festival than other screendance festivals? What types of non–Western dance forms may be represented in an international pool of submissions where people are coming into contact with the festival most often through the open platform of social media?

Upon looking at the submission pool geographically, I found many countries represented including Japan, Tunisia, Italy, Canada, Mexico, Germany, and several countries in South America. However the largest contingent of films comes from the United States. Like my previous analyses, I tallied demographic information for films with American origins only. One notable departure from the two previous analyses is that so many of the films submitted had no credits included in their final edits, so it seemed only fair to concern my analysis only with that which could be seen on screen as I would not be able to get an accurate tally of those working behind the camera. Although many of the films submitted appeared to be self-filmed, there were many where it was not completely clear whether the subjects were being seen through their own efforts or through the lens of someone else. It was also not clear in all films where the choreography originates. A good number of the films appeared to have improvised movement, but because this cannot be confirmed without written credits or speaking to each submitting artist, I could not make assumptions. As you can see, there are many differences evident between the Mobile Dance Film Festival and other more traditional festivals. It would seem that the use of mobile devices renders ownership—as it is most commonly communicated on the screendance festival circuit through the use of formal credits and websites dedicated to the work—much less important than projects made under circumstances that may indicate higher stakes for the work. Initially, this lack of claim was encouraging. "How lovely," I thought, "that perhaps when it is made clear that all are welcome, staking claim to that which is created in service of a shared space (social media or, in the case of the

MDFF, an extension of our collective digital experience through the smart-phone) is no longer a necessity for the work to exist and be recognized." Then I started to dig deeper.

When looking more deeply into the question of site, it became clear that the influence of the phone as a public object meant that many of the films were made outside in heavily-trafficked areas. As I watched the films, I wondered in particular about the politics of public space as they apply to various bodies as they move through these spaces. Take, for example, a film titled *New York Moment* (2019) by Andrew Harper and Katherine Henly. This film was selected for the 2019 festival and features two white perform-ers, a man and a woman, dancing their way through New York City as cap-tured by twenty-one camera operators including the filmmakers credited for the making of the film in addition to people who appear to be both tourists and city-dwellers. The dancers, Zoe Warshaw and Richard Walters, dressed in bright, primary colors, move with beautiful precision through the streets and subway station. They appear as either the main focus or in the background of shots that also feature tiny snippets of commentary by those operating the cameras. The film seems to capture some of the best parts of New York City as they exist in popular imagination: the "melting pot" of its inhabitants and visitors, the architecture, the buzz, the sights and sounds of a bustling cultural center. However when one stops to think about how street performers have been targeted and treated in New York City and other metropolitan areas, one wonders whether these dancers are operating with a level of privilege in this public space that others—specifically those who come from marginalized communities where their presence as artists in public may draw suspicion—do not possess. For example, the Litefeet dancers on the subway, those young men and women who perform impres-sive, acrobatic choreographies inside and outside of the subway cars, are often warned and sometimes arrested by police cracking down on street performers soliciting subway passengers for money and endangering the safety of riders as they dance. While the dancers in *New York Moment* were not asking for money as they danced through the crowds of New York City, would they have been stopped, warned, or arrested if they had? Couldn't it be argued that anyone dancing among crowds of people that are not danc-ing themselves may be considered "reckless endangerment," especially if an accident occurs where a dancing body unintentionally comes into contact with a non-dancing body? Though this was an unexpected aspect of the analysis that does not address my initial questions listed at the beginning of this case study, it is an important consideration as more collectivist festivals and social media platforms encourage public filmmaking. Especially where an obvious societal power dynamic exists, such as in the case where artists from developed or affluent areas of our country or the world make public films in underdeveloped or under-resourced areas (which was another recurring trope in the MDFF submission pool), it should be our job as a community of artists, curators, and presenters to become aware of when our pursuits become patronizing or otherwise harmful to others.

To my first question posed at the beginning of this case study, it turns out that the demographics as they relate to people seen on screen as performers found in the submission pool to the 2019 Mobile Dance Film Festival for American submissions are surprisingly *less* diverse than those of the 2019 ADF's Movies by Movers film festival. Where the total percentage of performers of color on screen as seen in the submission pool to ADF's Movies by Movers was tallied at about 34 percent, the same group tallied for the MDFF is about 25 percent. Male of color performers accounted for the least visible group on screen for both festivals in 2019 (MDFF, 7 percent, ADF's MBM, 13 percent). The largest discrepancy, though, was that concerning the split between male-presenting and female-presenting performers on screen. Eighty-two percent of the bodies seen on screen in American submissions to the Mobile Dance Film Festival were women. Seventy-one percent of the bodies seen in American submissions to ADF's Movies by Movers were women. A similarly large split occurred between the festivals with regard to white women specifically. White women as seen in the American submissions to the Mobile Dance Film Festival account for 64 percent, while those to ADF's Movies by Movers were tallied at 50 percent. One of the things that remains consistent between the two festivals with regard to the five years of data culled for the ADF's Movies by Movers film festival is the ubiquity of the white, female body—most expressly that of the conventionally beautiful, white, female body as seen on screen.

Performers 2019

White Female Performers	Women of Color Performers	White Male Performers	Male of Color Performers
MDFF: 64%	18%	11%	7%
MBM: 50%	21%	16%	13%

Total Women Performers for MDFF: 82%

Total Men Performers for MDFF: 18%

Total White Performers for MDFF: 75%

Total People of Color Performers for MDFF: 25%

Screendance from Film to Festival

Total Women Performers for MBM: 71%   Total White Performers for MBM: 66%
Total Men Performers for MBM: 29%   Total People of Color Performers for
                                              MBM: 34%

Anecdotally, the treatment of the female body on screen was consistent with that of ADF's Movies by Movers in that a vast majority of the bodies were young bodies (while I did not tally for age specifically, I would say that there were more young bodies on screen overall than in ADF's Movies by Movers). In the case of the Mobile Dance Film Festival, this may have something to do with the use of smartphones as the main apparatus for filmmaking. While the use of such devices certainly does not preclude older generations of artists from participating in the making of material in this vein, those more accustomed to filmmaking with other types of equipment may not necessarily feel the need to make the switch, or see the utility in creating work with smartphones.

In mining the submissions as a whole for non–Western dance forms, I did not see the breadth that I had assumed I would encounter. The vast majority of films, no matter where they were coming from, seemed to utilize a post-modern or improvisatory aesthetic to the exclusion of other recognizable forms of dance. Hip hop was employed recognizably a handful of times, as was ballet, but there was a perceptible dearth of films made to showcase dances as representations of particular cultures. One film that stood out for its uses of non–Western dance is *Soufisme* by Younes Ben Hajria. Listed as being Tunisian in origin, the film takes place in a wool processing and dying facility where the movements of the people working with the wool is captured as they lift and transport wool, work the machines, and otherwise move through the space. A single dancer, sometimes multiplied on screen, performs a Sufi whirling dervish dance in what appears to be an empty cistern or grain bin.

It would seem that in this way, both stylistically and demographically, there is a reliance on the international scope of a festival to bolster diversity (this goes for all festivals analyzed). And even though the organizers in each instance demonstrate a commitment to diversity, the challenge of making this a reality each season is one not easily surmounted when the landscape seems to be less diverse than we would like. How can the screendance community see diversity and inclusion on the circuit not as an exoticized "other," but as part and parcel of the screendance spectrum that invites a global participation because it is truly a diverse community?

With regard to the question of professional and non-professional bodies seen on screen in the 2019 submission pool to the Mobile Dance Film

Festival, there were some that appeared not to have had much experience with dance as it is usually understood and deployed on the screendance festival circuit. However, the vast majority of performers, even those few who may be described as students or hobbyists, were versed enough to show clear connections to the world of concert dance. This trend continues to demonstrate screendance's bias toward the dance part of its hybridity, where filmmaking runs the risk of being considered second to the movement.

After completing data and qualitative analysis of the 2019 season, I was fortunate to not only be granted access to the 2020 season submissions, but because of the enthusiastic curiosity and support of Andrew Chapman, I had a co-researcher for the first time in my efforts. Sitting down together over Zoom, we looked at and tallied all of the films with American origins and scanned the entire pool for trends and anomalies. The numbers for the 2020 season of the Mobile Dance Film Festival were different than the 2019 season, with a marked reduction in white female performers and a jump in the number of men of color performers. Once again, this occurred because of the presence of one film that had twenty-four Black men featured and not because of a more even distribution of performers of color across the pool. In the first line of the table below, I express percentages for the festival as it was tallied *with* the film that featured the large group of Black, male performers. In the second line, I express the data *without* the film to demonstrate how one film completely changes the numbers but tells a very different story of the diversity of the pool upon closer look.

Performers 2020

White Female Performers	Women of Color Performers	White Male Performers	Male of Color Performers
MDFF: 63%	11%	6%	20%
*MDFF: 72%	13%	7%	8%

*Without film with 24 Black men.

Total Women Performers for MDFF: 74%

Total Men Performers for MDFF: 26%

Total White Performers for MDFF: 69%

Total People of Color Performers for MDFF: 31%

Screendance from Film to Festival

*Total Women Performers for
MDFF: 85%
*Total Men Performers for MDFF:
15%

*Total White Performers for MDFF:
79%
*Total People of Color Performers
for MDFF: 21%

Stylistically, the submissions were similar to the previous year, with a mixture of films that were improvisatory, those that occurred in public, and a handful that were produced to a level that showed a high level of experience in the form. Again, there was an overall lack of forms of dance that could be considered a departure from post-modern aesthetics. Still, the Mobile Dance Film Festival remains an important facet of the screendance festival landscape that is helping to expand definitions of what screendance includes. As the festival continues to grow, opportunities for continued efforts to reach more artists and their work mean the potential for true distinction on the circuit. Of the experience, Chapman said:

> The submission data collected for the Mobile Dance Film Festival highlights that our work towards equitable representation in the field of Mobile Dance Filmmaking is ongoing. This study has redirected our understanding of what we considered easily accessible filmmaking helping us to focus on the filmmaking communities that are continuously, statistically underrepresented.

* * *

As I conclude this chapter, it is helpful to briefly touch on the curatorial outcomes of the three festivals that have had their submission pools analyzed before delving more deeply into questions of curation and inclusion broadly. For ADF's Movies by Movers, the five years in question have yielded varied levels of diversity on the program for each season. While overall the make-up of the people seen on screen and working behind the camera in the pieces chosen as official selections is often akin to those found in the data presented, there has been attention to diversity in the offerings such that many of the individual screenings found throughout the five years demonstrate an intentional mitigation of issues of representation and visibility. Some of these efforts have already been described in the section on curation. The same could be said for The Outlet Dance Project and the Mobile Dance Film Festival—in both festivals there can be identified places where the efforts of the curatorial teams are plainly evident in the selections. However, the overall outcomes of the festival programs show pitfalls where representation is concerned. For example, when considering diversity in the 2020 selected works for the Mobile Dance Film Festival, almost all are non–American films, reinforcing the notion that non–American equals diversity. In the selections to ADF's Movies by Movers in several seasons, there are screenings that, for example, highlight experimental dance films, and those are almost always mostly white directors, choreographers, and performers. While it would be sensible to point to the obvious representational challenges across the field as part of the reason, this could also be an issue of size, where the largest screendance festivals in the United States (the Dance on Camera Festival and San Francisco Dance Film Festival among them) may find more ease in creating parity among their selections due to larger submission pools, institutional relationships that yield connections to varied communities, and the overall reach of their marketing and events. The San Francisco Dance Film Festival, for example, shows a higher level of diversity in its offerings than all three of the festivals I analyzed in this chapter with regard to their selected works. However, for the 2019 season, they solicited no less than 15 percent of their selected works, which is a higher percentage than most. The relationships the San Francisco Dance Film Festival has with entities that produce films by and featuring diverse artists, like KQED,[3] is evident and could be used as inspiration for festivals of all sizes to cultivate organizational partnerships that can help to bolster diversity in their offerings.

As a conclusion to this work on representation in screendance, I take up the challenge of creating parity through curatorial activities on the part of screendance festivals across the United States in the next chapter. Through a collection of mini-case studies that show various models of operation and curation, Chapter 11 seeks to highlight the work curatorial teams and other staff and board members are doing to increase diversity and mitigate bias.

CHAPTER 11

Curatorial Considerations

Now that the challenges to equitable and considerate representation of makers and performers of screendance on the screendance festival circuit have been examined, I could not conclude my exploration of these issues without accounting for how festival directors and curators across the field are tackling these challenges creatively, with an eye toward the future. Though it is certain that there is much work to be done to achieve the kind of landscape that honors voices, bodies, dance genres, and aesthetic approaches to screendance making from a variety of backgrounds and philosophical foundations, the solutions presented in this chapter offer us hope and a collection of roadmaps to get there. These are two very important things.

Although the vast majority of this chapter was printed in the 2018 edition of the *International Journal of Screendance*,[1] I felt it important to present this information alongside the previous two chapters as a way of stitching together a complete and cohesive discussion of representation in the field. My hope is that these three chapters taken together will inspire those who watch, make, and program screendance to think more deeply about how our encounters with screendance can be a positive force in the world. In the mini-case studies included in this chapter, the directors and curators demonstrate their unique approaches to the quest for equitable representation in the field.

* * *

Moving Body–Moving Image Festival (New York, New York)

When Gabri Christa initiated the first Moving Body–Moving Image Festival in 2018, she did it out of a sense of exasperation at her observation that screendance festivals she had been in the habit of attending did not show much diversity on screen and felt unfocused with regard to curatorial thesis.

Chapter 11. Curatorial Considerations

Going to screendance festivals first with my own films and often ... my film being the only film with people of color, I started thinking about representation. That was over ten years ago. Then I started going to screendance festivals like Cinedanse, the bigger [festivals] and feeling dissatisfied with how much it felt all over the place for me [curatorially]. The idea for the Moving Body–Moving Image Festival actually started when I was artistic director and curator at Snug Harbor Cultural Center. I was making all these artistic programs and I started wondering, "If I would do a screendance festival, what would it look like?"

As mentioned earlier in the book, as a Collectivist-era festival, Christa's festival is a curatorial thesis in and of itself. The inaugural festival was publicized as "a festival exploring the depiction of the moving brown body in film." And from that thesis, two programs of films, an installation by dancer/visual artist Ayo Janeen Jackson and a conversation on the body of color in film between Oscar-nominated producer Lisa Cortes and Bessie Award–winning dance critic Eva Yaa Asantewaa materialized. Of the films screened during the festival, some standouts include a short documentary featuring tap dancer Fred Nelson titled *He Who Dances on Wood* (2017), directed by Jessica Beshir. Nelson hears rhythm in the world around him and experiences immense joy as a result. Cameron Thompkins' *This Black* (2017) is described by the director as a "film rooted in the physical and psychological struggles that come from not being able to safely express the range of human emotion

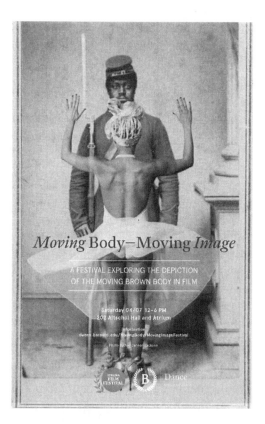

Promotional still from the inaugural Moving Body–Moving Image Festival, founded and directed by Gabri Christa. Courtesy Gabri Christa.

171

without triggering a stereotype or endangering an opportunity" where dancers Thompkins, Esosa Oviasu, and Edson Maldonado dance in and out of tenderness, conflict, delight and allusions to violence. David Rousseve's 2012 film *Two Seconds After Laughter* is based on Javanese choreographer's Sri Susilowati's experience of leaving her home country to be a dancer in the United States and explores concepts of memory, separation, and dislocation through traditional Indonesian dance.

The 2020 festival, titled *Aging and Othering*, explores the aging body in dance. For this iteration of the festival especially, it was important to have a curatorial team that could consider the films objectively from various generational standpoints.

> My curatorial team is a representation of the people that are going to be represented ... in this one [The Aging Body] I have two people in their seventies, one in their twenties, one in their thirties, myself, you know, forties, fifties so we get a much more intergenerational look at the films [for 2020].

Christa goes on to explain that collecting films featuring and about the aging body is more difficult than collecting films featuring and about the moving Brown body, though this was challenging as well. She notes that a challenge of soliciting films on a platform like FilmFreeway is that people often do not pay attention to the specifics of the call. In pre-screening submissions, Christa realized many of the films were unusable as they did not align with the curatorial thesis. At first, submissions were free, but soon Christa and her team were overrun with submissions. In instituting a $5 submission fee, the deluge of films was somewhat mitigated, but still presented a challenge in sifting through submissions to find films that could be considered at all for the festival. This experience demonstrates the desperation with which many artists look for outlets for their work in the midst of financial strain. Beyond that, Christa notes that the films that were not in keeping with the stated aims of the festival fell into dominant aesthetics and representational trends as demonstrated in the data presented earlier, "young, white women dancing on camera."

San Francisco Dance Film Festival (San Francisco, California)

At the time of this writing, Judy Flannery is the artistic director of the San Francisco Dance Film Festival, which was founded by Greta Schonberg in 2010. She says that one of the challenges to curating a program each year that shows all of the diversity to be found in dance film is that one cannot control what comes through the submission process. For example, she notes that submissions for 2017 were much more ballet-centric than previous years:

> We try to work with just the submissions, but we find sometimes that we just don't have the content that supports our philosophy of diversity in styles, genres and artists. We want to support this field and we want to embrace it in all its glorious diversity. So when we're not getting as many films that support our philosophy, we will make a conscious decision to go out and seek films that will fill a void we have.

While it is not uncommon for curators to actively seek films for their programs, Flannery makes it clear that she is a champion of non-traditional approaches to dance genres and enjoys presenting films that go against the status quo in terms of casting. Flannery states, "This art form will help people see outside of normal—outside of the box. That's why this art form should be celebrated. I think we have a duty as a festival to say, 'you need to show diversity!'"

Flannery also expresses the importance of supporting the local arts community, which adds to the inclusivity of the festival. "I noticed that we were getting a lot of films from Europe and New York," she says. In 2013, the San Francisco Dance Film Festival started the Co-Laboratory, a collaborative initiative for San Francisco–area dancers and filmmakers that pairs artists who have never worked together before and provides them with resources, screen time during the festival, and opportunities to have their work shown on touring reels that go to community partners. As a result, long-term artistic relationships are often forged, and artists can support each other in their making. In addition, the festival often pairs local, live dance groups with screened work for multi-faceted events that draw audiences that may choose to support the artists at other events. A good example of this practice was the screening of *Shake the Dust* in 2017, a hip-hop documentary. The SFDFF collaborated with the San Francisco Hip-Hop Festival and had live performance in conjunction with the screening of the film. Flannery sites similar collaborations with lindy hop, contemporary, ballet and other dance groups whose practices are rooted in styles from around the world.

When it comes to audiences, the San Francisco Dance Film Festival is equally as active in cultivating rich dialogue around issues of inclusion and inviting many facets of the community to the festival's events both within the regular season and year-round in between submission cycles.

Most notably, the festival engages partners in the community in conjunction with films that are screened, inviting non-artists to dialogue with artists, and vice-versa. For example, in 2016, the festival screened Frances McElroy's acclaimed documentary *Black Ballerina*. In preparation for the screening, SFDFF asked patrons to buy blocks of tickets that were then offered to groups of children from public schools, dance studios, and community centers and other places where young people of color are taking dance. The screening included a guest appearance by San Francisco Ballet dancer Kimberly Marie Oliver, who presented the film and assisted in leading a discussion after the film.

My interview with Flannery brings up one of the points that inspired me to begin doing the work of collecting demographics for ADF's Movies by Movers in the first place. As people are *self-selecting* to submit to our festivals, this information gives us insight into who is most readily able to create and disseminate work. It gives us information about stylistic trends happening in the concert dance and media worlds, and how select voices are privileged within those trends. Most importantly, this information calls into question what our role is as curators and programmers. As Flannery points out, it is our job to actively seek films that highlight the work of less visible groups and styles of dance.

Unique among many festivals in the United States is the Co-Laboratory that Flannery describes, a rare opportunity in the screendance community for artists to be supported through networking and commission. The reason this type of program is so rare is that many of the festivals aren't able to support this type of program financially. Again, issues of a lack of industry affect our ability to be better stewards of this art form. While the San Francisco Dance Film Festival also struggles financially—none of the festivals described in this piece do not in some way—the Co-Laboratory and other programs that bolster the local arts community are prioritized in ways that compel the festival's organizers to forge strong community partnerships which help this and other outreach programs to be sustainable.

Sans Souci Festival of Dance Cinema (Boulder, Colorado)

David Leserman and Michelle Bernier of the Sans Souci Festival of Dance Cinema in Boulder, Colorado, agree that there are challenges to curating in the midst of a time when so much content is available on the internet and many people simply choose not to submit to festivals. Because part of their mission is to introduce audiences to screendance and to educate them about the art form, in the curatorial process they often curate programs that are not representative of the demographic landscape of screendance that they observe. Bernier says:

> Part of me feels like there's dance cinema, then there's all the dance that you see on the internet and TV. A lot of our audience doesn't look at this [screendance] any differently than they look at that [mass media]. Too, they can see different people dancing on screen on the internet. They don't have to see how biased things are and how frankly, white-washed things are. In dance film, I think that there is the same bias [as mass media] but on a smaller scale, and we can actually do something so it doesn't look that way when we put a show out. That's the way I think about it. You know our submissions may be whatever, say, as a guess, 80 percent white—it doesn't mean what we show has to be 80 percent white. And because that's what happens in Hollywood and that's what happens on *So You Think You Can Dance*, that's what happens in all the other screendance that they get, dance cinema might be another good place to remind people that, "oh, that's not actually all there is out there," even though that may feel like we are giving an unfair representation of what the field looks like. I actually think that's totally ok. I think that if you're coming here for cultural enrichment, just go smorgasbord style. And let's just do a little bit of everything.

Bernier and Leserman believe in the practice of honesty when confronting new material and not turning away from their areas of unfamiliarity. Leserman readily acknowledges that there are areas where he may fall short with regard to diversity. "There are cultural differences that I don't feel the least bit qualified to make a judgment about. I don't always have the cultural underpinnings to recognize something as valuable."

In the curatorial process, Leserman points out that inclusivity and sensitivity to varied subject matter can be cultivated by having people from marginalized groups on the curatorial team:

> I have a bias toward diversity because I'm a disabled dancer. I danced actively for about ten years in a wheelchair as a mature person. And so I never did perform in a dance in any way before I did it in a wheelchair. And so I'm consciously biased towards disability-related dance and we usually show one if we get one. We usually get one every year.

Leserman goes on to note that the founder of Sans Souci and fellow curator Ana Baer is of Mexican descent and that she brings more sensitivity to the table around race and non–Western dance.

Bernier then points to the reality that there are times in the curatorial process when they question their ability to make a judgment on whether something they've received is culturally sensitive or not as a work of art:

We do run into this issue sometimes, where we feel unqualified to say, "Does this feel like an accurate representation of a thing?" because we are talking too about how we want to assume that every artist that submits something to the festival is also fully qualified to make a statement about the thing they're making a statement about. I want to respect the artists and I want to err on the side that everything the artist does is an artistic choice.

With these acknowledgments, both Leserman and Bernier consider the choice to have a curatorial team of several people from varied backgrounds, both personally and professionally, a way to mitigate some of their individual pitfalls. Bernier says that solo curating would make the program "heavy-handed." And Leserman and Bernier talk about how conversations about diversity and intersectionality have come up organically in their deliberations as a result of their model of working.

The curatorial team at Sans Souci demonstrates the necessity of dialogue between people of various backgrounds and viewpoints in curation. Through this kind of collaborative curation, we can better understand that issues of representation aren't just about one thing. Issues of race, gender, class, education, ability—they're all intertwined, and in the context of screendance, we have an opportunity to influence how audiences encounter and understand these concepts aesthetically. While each of the Sans Souci curators may not individually be able to fully consider the cultural and aesthetic aspects of the films they receive and ultimately choose to screen, the three of them together can better do the work of creating diverse experiences for their audiences. As a part of the mission of Sans Souci is to introduce and educate audiences about screendance, it is important that the curators recognize how their conversations in the curatorial process influence what audiences may leave with after their first screendance experience. Having had the pleasure of attending the Sans Souci festival in September 2017, I can attest to the fact that the team stays true to their mission, creating for the audience a multi-faceted experience through multimedia performance, films featuring a variety of dance forms, people, and production values.

Dance on Camera Festival (New York, New York)

Co-curator Liz Wolff says that the Dance on Camera Festival benefits greatly from being situated in New York City, with such a long history. "We have a very open market; the submissions are far and wide and incredibly varied. We benefit from that cross selection," she says, and notes that while she hasn't had the experience of curating in other markets, she's happy to be doing work in one that invites such diversity because it's already understood that New York is a cultural and artistic melting pot.

Even so, the Dance Films Association and the Dance on Camera Festival are known for attention to detail in their programming, pairing sought-after feature-length films with innovative and lesser-known short films, curating shorts programs with a similar mixture of known and unknown talent, collaborating with community partners, and creating space for engaged dialogue throughout the festival. In comparison to many other festivals around the country, the amount of opportunities for discussion with artists and field experts brings an added dimension to the festival. Of the myriad discussion experiences offered throughout the festival, Wolff says, "We choose work for that reason—to have a conversation—whether it's about social inequities, differently-abled bodies ... we keep an eye out to make sure we're having a full conversation ... we definitely delve into open forum discussions, so we're not just showing a film if we feel it needs discussion.... Our job is to translate art to the audience."

Something that both supports Dance on Camera in having those successful conversations about the films they program and that sets the festival apart from other festivals is its relationship and collaboration with the Film Society of Lincoln Center, which co-presents Dance on Camera. Through relationships cultivated across the Center's wide range of programming, it provides access to potential audience members throughout the five boroughs, and beyond. Wolff explains how this relationship translates into targeted audiences:

> They have contacts to work with the community at large—inviting different groups like the School for the Blind [for the 2017 screening of *Looking at the Stars*, about the Fernanda Bianchini Ballet Association for the Blind in São Paulo], reaching out into the tri-borough area—even if it's something like a New York City Ballet piece and the School of American Ballet is upstairs, something we can offer the students—if we find there's a special program that needs special attention, we have a way to help bring in audience.

Again, Wolff recognizes this relationship as a benefit to the festival that festivals in smaller markets may not enjoy.

With a reputation for some of the most varied dance film programming among the dance film community, Dance on Camera's outreach efforts achieve similarly high standards. Capturing Motion is a program in collaboration with the NYC Department of Education that engages high school students throughout the five boroughs in creating dance films that are then entered into the Capturing Motion annual competition. Winners have their work screened at Dance on Camera. Through the process of workshop to production and submission, students get to learn about the process of creating a film and working to get it screened. Wolff says, "What you get from these kids is pretty incredible. Capturing Motion gives them an opportunity to express themselves differently. The Department of Education in New York City has a deep dive into the arts in schools, and Capturing Motion is that marriage of filmmaking and dance."

Finally, the Dance Films Association regularly collaborates with other curators and organizations to curate and present varied screenings throughout the year. Partners in recent years have included ADF's Movies by Movers, Trikselion Arts, DCTV, and more. By opening up a dialogue and collaborating on programming efforts, the Dance Films Association helps to keep the conversation percolating about curation, new work, diversity, screendance and mainstream culture, and how to keep advancing the art of screendance.

The Dance Films Association in many ways exemplifies how a long-established organization can bolster the screendance community as a whole. Situated in a long-standing artistic center, a balance of well-known and lesser-known artists, community partnerships, partnerships with other screendance presenters and organizations, a commitment to the history and preservation of screendance, availability of their material for other presenters to share, production grants for artists, and a platform from which the organization can garner diverse audiences all speak to why Dance on Camera has lasted so long where other screendance initiatives have perished. Unique about Dance on Camera, though, is its relationship with the Department of Education. No other festival representatives I interviewed (and very few across the country) have programs for young filmmakers. Indeed, creating opportunities for youth in such a diverse place as the five boroughs of New York will have positive dividends as those young people become adults, making art in the world.

Tiny Dance Film Festival (San Francisco, California)

Kat Cole, a co-curator of the Tiny Dance Film Festival in San Francisco says that in the spirit of accessibility, she and co-curator Eric Garcia are champions of do-it-yourself films and do not place as high a priority on production value as other festivals might. Because of this, the Tiny Dance Film Festival gets to celebrate the emergence of newer, more accessible technologies, and show films that would be unlikely choices at larger festivals. As a commitment to accessibility for submitting artists, the price for submissions has remained low since the festival's inception, at only $5. This price is well below the price asked by most of the festivals operating in the United States today. For Cole and Garcia, the DIY spirit breaks the pattern of films that fall within a particular realm of representation and allows for a more fluid definition of the art form of screendance. "For example," Cole says, "there's these two young dancers and they've made a film about race with Barbie dolls, and it's really fun!" And it is films like this one Cole describes which sets the Tiny Dance Film Festival apart from some of the larger festivals and gives Tiny Dance its signature quirk.

According to Cole and Garcia, their particular brand of aesthetic boundary-stretching and definition blurring means that for the Tiny Dance Film Festival, intersectional programming is a "consciousness that is organic to our own progression as artists." Detour Dance is the name of the dance company that acts as the umbrella for Tiny Dance and boasts a roster of work that is socio-politically and community engaged. As people who both identify as people of color and queer, Cole and Garcia actively encourage people of color, queer people and others who belong to marginalized groups to send work to the festival.

Cole says, "We want to showcase folks that are operating on the outskirts of contemporary dance, of film, of media representation in general. I feel like there is something significant in seeing those bodies on screen, that I always feel good about."

What the Tiny Dance Film Festival makes most clear is that the screendance community needs spaces that champion and screen work that does not generally find a place at other festivals where the expectations for production value and virtuosity are high. The projects Cole and Garcia look for are expressions of experimentalism that challenge the white, patriarchal experimentalism of performance art history that our genre is tied to.[2] The need for queer, people of color voices to help the community be introduced to other queer, people of color voices and other marginalized groups is invaluable. While the issue of marginalized people supporting and disseminating the work of other marginalized people has long raised questions of whether or not it is still the job of those people to see, appreciate, and share the value of work they make for non-marginalized communities, it is clear that the work Garcia and Cole are doing with the Tiny

Dance Film Festival makes the screendance community a more equitable one.

* * *

Although these conversations represent just a handful of festivals with a handful of solutions to offer, it is clear that there are curators for whom questions of diversity are front and center in their deliberations. Things like clear curatorial goals, diverse curatorial teams, community partnerships, community outreach, and opportunities for artists are great ways to help the screendance landscape become more inclusive. Festivals like the ones explored here and others not mentioned can act as examples of how to make inclusion an important aspect of the curatorial process for those interested in starting new screendance festivals, or those who are looking to imbue their existing festivals with more socio-cultural context. One thing that was not mentioned in any of the interviews, though, is confronting the exclusionary histories as they are written in our literature. I have already troubled these histories some by mentioning the first Black dancers on film—tap dancers Joe Rastus, Denny Tolliver, and Walter Wilkins as captured by the Edison Company in 1894—in the first chapter of this book. The Edison Company was also responsible for one of the first films with a queer aesthetic, titled *Gay Brothers*, filmed in 1895 and featuring two men engaged in a ballroom dance together. In 1910, the Foster Photoplay Company was founded, the first Black-owned film house in the United States, which produced the 1913 film, *The Railroad Porter*, featuring famous vaudevillian Burt Williams. The film, which did not survive physically, featured a full-cast cakewalk, a very popular American dance form derived from African American dances on Southern plantations in the 1800s. The mid–20th century also offers us gems: African American filmmaker Julie Dash, famous for works like *Daughters of the Dust* (1991) and *The Rosa Parks Story* (2002), made *Four Women* in 1975, a screendance featuring dancer/choreographer Linda Martina Young dancing to Nina Simone's song of the same name. This little-talked-about screendance won major awards, including Best Women's Film at the 1977 Miami International Film Festival. In 1980, Shirley Clarke made a lesser-known film, *A Visual Diary*, featuring African American performer Blondell Cummings in a captivating performance of emotional turmoil. The years 1985 to 1993 offer us Nuyorican[3] artist Raphael Montañez Ortiz and his "Dance Series" of dance films created by cutting together snippets of old Hollywood films to create repetitious, rhythmic dances for the screen. *Dance Number 22* (1993) won the Grand Prix at the 1993 international Locarno Video Festival in Switzerland. The year 1998 brings us Ruth Sergel's *Bruce*, a film with a multicultural production team that features Black, disabled dancer Bruce Jackson. The film traveled to several film festivals and was broadcast on PBS. The early 2000s also feature some lesser-known history—Baz Luhrmann's *Moulin Rouge* is released in 2001 and is heavily influenced by the dances and aesthetics of Bollywood.

This small disruption to the existing histories of screendance is hardly exhaustive! A full reframing of this history would warrant a whole other book. Nevertheless, a short excavation such as this works to illuminate areas of obscurity in our history and helps us to come to terms with the ways we have intentionally and unintentionally erased the voices of members of our community, and do better moving forward!

I do believe it is now time to present what I consider to be the climax of this work. After the years spent working on this book, immersing myself in the history of the screendance festival, charting lineages and making connections between the filmic and fine arts, and cultivating a deeper relationship to my curatorial practice, it felt only natural to write a manifesto. Perhaps, in the tradition of those artist collectives who penned manifestoes in the past, this is an encapsulation of philosophy for the purpose of laying claim to some way of being in the world. Of course, I'm no Marinetti in that my goal is not alienation. Rather, I wish to issue an invitation. I invite you, dear reader, to read and to absorb what follows. As you do, I invite you to agree, disagree, feel ambivalence, draft your own statement, write a book, make a film, make fun, scoff, revel, and read, read, read some more. It is always worth remembering that no matter the platform—be it institutional, community, or otherwise—that the reason we come to the arts is because art, and more specific to this book, screendance, is a place for visioning.

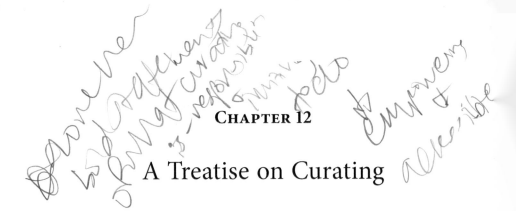

CHAPTER 12

A Treatise on Curating

In recognition of the inherent humanness of creativity in a realm recognized as "art" as a response to the experience of the natural world and the structures humans cultivate therein; of the human penchant for critical response to artistic works and the categorization and archive of those works; and of the human inclination for the cultivation of space for housing precious objects and ideas, I dive deep into the theoretical and embodied experience of acting as a liaison between artists, their objects, and their spectators, community co-conspirators, and critics, for the purpose of articulating what it means to curate—to care for artistic work that is not my own. In my explication, I attempt to express the work of curating as a multiplicity of meaning and action, tethered by a singular desire to uphold the integrity of art as it is presented to me by the artist and the desire for that work to have a life beyond its initial invention. In honor of these recognitions and desires, I present the following as a declaration of my personal beliefs born of my practice and experiences and as a call to action to those who identify as curators of screendance for deeper consideration of our work as a philosophical and technical pursuit both separate from and necessary to the health and proliferation of screendance. In light of my intention to be clear in my aspirations and commitments, I profess the following to be true:

Curating is a radical act of communication.

It is a way of cultivating and caring for an environment where art and artists can be in critical dialogue with other art and artists, with audiences and with society. It is a way of creating containers for the art to exist in— not physical containers per se, but metaphorical containers. Contextual containers. Thematic containers. Each container has the opportunity to be a unique platform for the work to be considered and reconsidered by both the audience and the artist. It is a way to create space for the artist to play, to ruminate, to dream, to experiment, and to grow. It is a way of supporting artists in placemaking: bringing an audience into a world invented through their creative pursuits with the support of an institution (institutions can include museums, art houses, universities, non-profits, community centers, a neighborhood, one's own home—I am using this term broadly here—an institution is wherever you decide it is … an institution can be *you* and whatever resources you have to give, including your time and attention). It is a way of making sense of seemingly disparate approaches to making and doing.

Curators are a conduit.

Curating is a way of inviting audiences and society at large to see the array of options available in thinking about and interacting with the world as demonstrated by the artist with the context to make those examples accessible and available.

Curating is a method of amplifying the artist's voice.

Curating offers us opportunities to "see what happens." What happens when two or more works are intentionally juxtaposed? What happens when there is a clear thematic through line in a collection of work? What happens if the audience is invited to interact directly with the work? What happens when art is presented out of context, or in the context of someone else's work? What happens when the audience is given important pieces of information before encountering the work? What happens when information is withheld until after the work has been encountered?

Curating is a constant deluge of questions.

It is our job to be curious.

Curating is a look across the landscape of our art form.

It is a way of understanding the times we live in, and how our time influences the art that gets made in the world. As a curator, one often gets to see the trajectory of the artist, as they make work over many months or years. From the vantage point of curation, we get to see the results of those artists wrestling with complex concepts, paying homage to the past, testing bold new ideas, staging tricky experiments, suffering failure and reveling in creative triumph. We are entrusted with their ritual objects.

Curating is a privilege.

Curating allows the curator to become familiar with the methods and techniques of the work, and how those things change over time. Eventually, we become much more than enthusiasts or champions. We become steeped in the culture of the art we curate. We get to comprehend the place and function of the art, as it is our duty to set the stage for the artist to share deeply and broadly. We cannot do that without deep and broad familiarity.

Curating is a way of knowing.

As curators, we see the breadth of the aesthetic landscape. Given this, it should be part of our practice to recognize when certain voices or approaches aren't being represented across our landscape and to be able to be creative in helping artists shift paradigms by listening to them when they provide us with new and important information by providing platforms for their work.

Curating is a way of creating space for diverse voices.

As a curators, we have the privilege of being invited into the world of each artist whose work we encounter, and we are whisked away into other worlds, colored by our own perceptions. It is through this process that we can begin to ask the question of what screendance *could* be. How many different ways can digital space reinvent itself?

Curating requires our full attention.

Curating requires time; curating should never be a rushed endeavor. This can be a challenge in today's fast-moving world and in the context of our festivals where the pressure to produce events often supersedes our need for time to deeply consider the "why" of our choices.

Curating requires openness.

Openness to allow the work to speak for itself. For curatorial possibilities to make themselves apparent to us, instead of letting perceptions limit the scope of what's possible. When soliciting submissions, as we do in a screendance festival, we are inviting the reality of chance into our curation. And in that chance comes the playful act of seeing what emerges.

Curating requires boundless enthusiasm.

This enthusiasm is especially necessary for those pieces that do not meet our personal aesthetic preferences. We have to be enthusiastic enough to be able to discover nuances and value where it may not be apparent to us upon first look.

Curators must be dreamers.

We have to be able to imagine a world where ideas and expression can actually change the trajectory of history, to imagine that art can change the world. As we dream of what art can do, we must dream of creating the environment for it to do its best work, then we must create it.

Chapter 12. A Treatise on Curating

Curating requires that we always be learning.

As technology changes, so should we. As socio-cultural overtures change, so should we. As the world becomes more connected, so should we.

Curating is an ethical pursuit.

A curator should be working to develop themselves as a steward. A curator should be concerned with the health and well-being of the art form and its makers.

A curator is a fierce advocate.

> "None of us exists in isolation. I think that's the great lesson of art. That we are immediately aware, always of the continuity of ideas that has existed from way, way back. So to me, it's the most concrete manifestation of the continuity of human understanding."—Nick Waterlow, Curator

Chapter Notes

Chapter 1

1. *Folding Over Twice* was screened at the 2009 Indie Grits Festival. I have since screened three other films at the festival (2010, 2011, 2019) with my film *Two Downtown* (2009) winning the Short Grit award at the 2010 festival. http://archive.indiegrits.org/2009-official-selections/.

2. The Dance:Film festival ceased operations in 2011. Not to be confused with the Screen.Dance festival begun in 2017 by Simon Fildes and also not to be confused with the ScreenDance Festival in Stockholm, Sweden, started in 2015!

Chapter 2

1. It has been suggested by some scholars that Djamille may have been born a man, which would make the censorship of her dance not only censorship of a woman on screen, but censorship of someone with queer or trans identity.

2. "Dada" is a title that has been the subject of conjecture among the inventors of Dada as to how it originated. It is also the title of the group's magazine, first published in 1917.

Chapter 3

1. "The first and most primitive method of recording television programs, production, or news story, a kinescope is a film made of a live television broadcast. Kinescopes are usually created by placing a motion picture camera in front of a television monitor and recording the image off the monitor's screen while the program is being aired. The recording method came into wide use around 1947" (Museum of Broadcast Communications, 2020).

2. *Dance Observer*, January 1949.

Chapter 4

1. Claudia Kappenberg presented this question at the American Dance Festival screendance symposium organized by Douglas Rosenberg in 2000.

2. Unpublished interview with Deirdre Towers, 2018.

3. In a 1953 letter to dancemaker Kurt Jooss, Langlois discusses the Cinémathèque's involvement with creating a film of the choreographer's work, *The Green Table*, for non-commercial use. It should be noted however, that this particular film was never produced.

4. It should be noted that film critic and scholar Nicolas Villodre disagrees with the BAMFA, though there is no physical evidence I found to either substantiate or refute this notion. As Meerson was a close confidante of Langlois, the possibility of the confluence of a prolonged relationship and the inherent exchange of ideas in such an arrangement may well have influenced the development of these events, even if only tangentially. http://archive.bampfa.berkeley.edu/film/FN10278.

5. While I had heard that the festival happened at least twice, the librarians at the DNC France confirmed that programs from the Dance Festival only show one year of programming that includes the dance film festival.

6. This language is from a pamphlet located in the home of cinephile and

187

historian Nicolas Villodre in Paris, France. It is the only piece of paraphernalia from the festival, and the only evidence of its existence I could find.

7. New York Public Library Archives.

8. Beenhakker's film *Wiped* won first prize at the Dance on Camera Festival in 2002. In one interview, current Cinedans director Martine Dekker is quoted as saying that she and Beenhakker attended a screendance festival in San Francisco in 2003. The San Francisco Dance Film Festival did not yet exist and I could find no evidence of any film being screened in San Francisco on his personal CV listed on his artist website. http://www.danshans.com/bio.html. https://movementexposed.com/2020/03/26/martine-dekker-cinedans/.

9. While there exists a clipping of the award announcement in the *New York Herald Tribune* in 1960, I did not come across a screening announcement for the project after its completion. This clipping is available for view at the New York Public Library Jerome Robbins Dance Library.

10. This newsletter was edited by Pauline Tish, Virginia Brooks, and Deirdre Towers at various times between the 1970s and 1990s.

11. Commentary in this chapter is from excerpts of unpublished interviews with members of the screendance community between 2017 and 2020.

12. Daniel Nagrin was the performer in Shirley Clarke's film, *Dancing in the Sun,* which was honored by the Dance Films Association in 1954.

13. Doris Totten Chase is famous for her colorful dance films and is considered one of the pioneers of 1970s video art.

14. Filmmaker known for his collaborations with avant-garde choreographer Merce Cunningham.

15. See Blas Payri's 2018 article, "Life and Death of Screendance Festivals: A Panorama," in the journal *Videodance Studies.*

16. 16 Sans Souci website.

17. Many of the second-generation festivals had content overlap in their programs, and anecdotally, several third-generation festival directors mentioned that one impetus for starting new festivals was because they didn't see themselves in existing ones.

Chapter 5

1. Though what the canon includes is debatable to some extent and dependent on the curators to offer definitions of what that includes.

2. EFV costs about $2,500 per person to participate. While artists are housed, they are expected to bring their own equipment. The program is subsidized through grants and in-kind resources, however. Sheppard estimates that the true cost of the program is somewhere near $10,000 per participant.

3. Moving 24 FPS costs about $30 to participate for the weekend.

4. Founded in 1994 as the Cucalorus Film Festival.

5. The Grounds for Sculpture is a 42-acre sculpture park founded in 1992. Its outdoor park features about 300 individual sculpture works while the indoor galleries feature rotating exhibitions.

6. This journal is the product of the videodance-studies gathering Pyari organizes. He and Rafel Arnal edited the 2018 edition of the journal.

Chapter 6

1. Unpublished interview, 2018.

2. For full nudity. I was hesitant because I had promised the owner of the venue where the event would take place that the screening would be family-friendly.

3. It could be argued that even in the most haphazard presentations, one can draw through lines and find juxtapositions if the art simply occurs in space, and this is indeed one approach to curating that exists in the curatorial ether.

Chapter 7

1. Modern dance and ballet on film and video catalogue members memo.

2. Though I did not see a catalogue published in 1979 in the NYPL archives, the second edition is dated 1980.

Chapter 9

1. Parts of this section first appeared in the *International Journal of Screendance,*

Vol. 8 and 9, and have been expanded in length and scope for this volume.

2. In another part of my life, I have been involved with diversity and inclusion efforts at the institutional level and have learned that demographic surveys are difficult to get people to take. While some studies on surveys show that incentivizing surveys does increase response, in this instance, I did not find that option to be a desirable or feasible one.

3. This is anecdotal, of course, but some of the conversations I have had with other festival directors have informed me that some do feel villainized by my efforts.

4. According to the U.S. Census, minorities make up nearly 40 percent of the population and are on track to become the majority by 2050. Hunt et al. references these numbers in the report.

5. See the letter to the National Endowment for the Arts penned by Yup'ik artist Emily Johnson in January 2021, explaining her experience with Peak Performances at Montclair State University. https://emily-72967.medium.com/a-letter-i-hope-in-the-future-doesnt-need-to-be-written-52e1d6fd5350.

6. *Dance* magazine ran an article in 2020 titled "This Ballet Company Will Only Dance Works by Women in 2020. The Director Doesn't Think That Should Be News," while the Hollywood Diversity Report noted a continual underrepresentation of women in positions of leadership and lead roles. Also, Linda Nochlin's 1971 essay "Why Have There Been No Great Women Artists?" is still in circulation as galleries and museums, both large and small, grapple with gender parity.

7. FilmFreeway synopsis.
8. FilmFreeway synopsis.
9. FilmFreeway description.

Chapter 10

1. From website. https://www.theoutletdanceproject.com/.

2. Stephanie Koontz' book, *The Way We Never Were,* discusses the construction of the perfect family in the media which included the nuclear, white, able-bodied, cisgender, hetero-normative family. Others were not considered "agreeable" characters.

3. KQED's *If Cities Could Dance* series features many underrepresented dancers and choreographers, and offerings from the series were featured in the SFDFF's 2019 season.

Chapter 11

1. "Curatorial Practices for Intersectional Programming" was published in the 2018 edition of the *International Journal of Screendance,* guest edited by Melissa Blanco Borelli and Raquel Monroe.

2. Erin Brannigan's book, *Dancefilm: Choreography and the Moving Image,* explores in depth the relationship of screendance to performance art. Additionally, RoseLee Goldberg's book, *Performance Art: From Futurism to Present,* highlights the many ways performance art is both subversive and elitist.

3. New Yorker of Puerto Rican heritage.

Bibliography

Abel, Ken. 1962. "Interview with Pauline Koner." Broadcast. New London, Connecticut, 91.5 FM.

Appolonio, Umbro. 1973. *Futurist Manifestos*. London: Thames and Hudson.

Arp, Hans. 1948. "Dadaland." 2021. http://www-personal.umich.edu/~ashaver/arp/1948/dadaland.html.

Balio, Tino. 2009. *United Artists: The Company Built by the Stars*. Madison: University of Wisconsin Press.

Balzer, David. 2015. *Curationism: How Curating Took Over the Art World and Everything Else*. London: Pluto Press.

Barber, Nicholas. 2016. "How Leni Riefenstahl Shaped the Way We See the Olympics." BBC Culture. BBC. Accessed March 1, 2021. https://www.bbc.com/culture/article/20160810-how-leni-riefenstahl-shaped-the-way-we-see-the-olympics.

Basquin, Kit Smyth. 2020. "Abstract Animation." Essay. In *Mary Ellen Bute: Pioneer Animator*, 27–76. New Barnet, UK: John Libbey Publishing.

Beardsley, Eleanor. 2018. "In France, The Protests of May 1968 Reverberate Today—And Still Divide The French." Episode. *Morning Edition*, NPR, May 29, 2018.

Berger, John. 1972. *Ways of Seeing, Episode 2*. YouTube. https://www.youtube.com/watch?v=mlGI8mNU5Sg&has_verified=1.

Berghaus, Günter and Aleš Erjavec. 2019. "The Politics of Futurism." Essay. In *Handbook of International Futurism*, 28–46. Berlin: De Gruyter.

Berghaus, Günter and Wanda Strauven. 2019. "Cinema." Essay. In *Handbook of International Futurism*, 101–15. Berlin: De Gruyter.

Bosma, Peter. 2015. *Film Programming: Curating for Cinemas, Festivals, Archives*. London: Wallflower Press.

Breton, André. 1934. "Matteson Art." *Andre Breton's "What Is Surrealism?" Matteson Art*. http://www.mattesonart.com/andre-bretons-what-is-surrealism-1934.aspx.

Bromberg, Ellen. 2000. "Archives of University of Utah International Screendance Festival." Salt Lake City: University of Utah.

Bute, Mary Ellen. 1934. *Rhythm in Light*. Film.

"Choreotones Dance Directors Air Views on Television Production." *Musical America*, April 1946.

CNN. 2020. "Over 1,300 Complaints Were Sent to the FCC about Shakira and J.Lo's Super Bowl Halftime Show." CBS58. https://www.cbs58.com/news/over-1-300-complaints-were-sent-to-the-fcc-about-shakira-and-jlos-super-bowl-halftime-show.

Conley, Katharine. 2013. "The Cinematic Whirl of Man Ray's Ghostly Objects." Essay. In *Surrealist Ghostliness*. Lincoln: University of Nebraska Press.

DanceBARN Collective. Accessed March 2, 2021. https://www.dancebarncollective.org/.

Dare to Dance in Public Film Festival (D2D). Accessed March 2, 2021. https://www.daretodanceinpublic.com/.

Davidson, Dave, director. 2013. *Hans Richter: Everything Turns Everything Revolves*.

Detour Dance. Accessed March 2, 2021. https://www.detourdance.com/.

Bibliography

De Valck, Marijke. 2007. *Film Festivals: From European Geopolitics to Global Cinephilia.* Amsterdam: Amsterdam University Press.

"Early Broadcast." Museum of Broadcast Communications. Accessed October 2020. https://museum.tv/.

Erigha, Maryann. 2019. *The Hollywood Jim Crow: The Racial Politics of the Movie Industry.* New York: New York University Press.

George, Adrian. 2015. *The Curator's Handbook: Museums, Commercial Galleries, Independent Spaces.* London: Thames & Hudson.

Gutierrez, Miguel. 2018. "Does Abstraction Belong to White People?" BOMB Magazine. https://bombmagazine.org/articles/miguel-gutierrez-1/.

Hagan, Cara. 2016. "The Feminist Body Reimagined in Two Dimensions: An Exploration of the Intersections Between Dance Film and Contemporary Feminism." *Dance's Duet with the Camera: Motion Pictures*, ed. Telory D. Arendell, Basingstoke: Palgrave Macmillan.

Hagan, Cara. 2017. "Visual Politics in American Dance Film: Representation and Disparity." *The International Journal of Screendance* 8. https://doi.org/10.18061/ijsd.v8i0.5360.

Hagan, Cara. 2018. "The Feminist Body Reimagined in Two Dimensions: An Exploration of the Intersections Between Dance Film and Contemporary Feminism." Essay. In *Dance's Duet with the Camera Motion Pictures*, edited by Telory D. Arendell and Ruth Barnes, 49–68. London: Palgrave Macmillan UK.

Hagener, Malte. 2014. "Institutions of Film Culture: Festivals and Archives as Network Nodes." Essay. In *The Emergence of Film Culture: Knowledge Production, Institution Building and the Fate of the Avant-Garde in Europe, 1919–1945,* edited by Malte Hagener, 283–305. New York ; Oxford: Berghahn.

Hunt, Darnell, Ana-Christina Ramon, and Michael Tran. 2019. *Hollywood Diversity Report: Old Story, New Beginning.* Los Angeles: UCLA.

Institute on Disability. 2020. *2019 ANNUAL REPORT ON PEOPLE WITH DISABILITIES IN AMERICA.* Durham, NH: University of New Hampshire.

Internet Movie Data Base (IMDB). "All Quiet on the Western Front." https://www.imdb.com/title/tt0020629/.

Internet Movie Data Base (IMDB). "West Side Story." https://www.imdb.com/title/tt0055614/.

Ivins, Laura. 2017. "Mathematical Beauty: Visual Music by Mary Ellen Bute." Indiana University Cinema. December 14, 2017. https://blogs.iu.edu/aplaceforfilm/2017/12/18/mathematical-beauty-visual-music-by-mary-ellen-bute/.

Koner, Pauline. 1993. "Inventing Dance for Television." *Dance Magazine* 67, no. 12 (December).

Koner, Pauline, and Kitty Doner. 1946. "The Technique of Dance in Television." *Telescreen* 5, no. 2 (January).

Koner, Pauline, and Kitty Doner. 1946. "Tele-Dance Talk." *Telescreen* 5, no. 2 (April).

Koner, Pauline, and Kitty Doner. 1947. "Tele-Dance." *Telescreen.*

Koner, Pauline, and Kitty Doner. 1949. "Television Dance." *Dance Observer* (January).

Kuoni, Carin. 2001. *Words of Wisdom: A Curator's Vade Mecum on Contemporary Art; on the Occasion of the 25th Anniversary of Independent Curators International (ICI), New York.* New York: Independent Curators International.

Langlois, Georges Patrick, and Glenn Myrent. 1995. *Henri Langlois, First Citizen of Cinema.* New York: Twayne.

Lobl, Muriel. 1970. "Dance Films Association." *Sightlines.*

Loiperdinger, Martin. 2004. "Lumière's 'Arrival of the Train': Cinema's Founding Myth." *The Moving Image: The Journal of the Association of Moving Image Archivists* 4, no. 1: 89–118. http://www.jstor.org/stable/41167150.

Marinetti, Filippo Tomasso. 1909. *The Futurist Manifesto.* Paris: Marinetti et al.

Marinetti, F.T. 1913. "The Founding Manifesto of Futurism." In Umbro Appolonio. 1973. *Futurist Manifestos.* London: Thames and Hudson, 19–24.

Bibliography

Marinetti, F.T. 1916. "The Futurist Cinema." In Umbro Appolonio. 1973. *Futurist Manifestos.* London: Thames and Hudson, 207–219.

Mathematical Beauty: Visual Music by Mary Ellen Bute. 2017. YouTube. https://www.youtube.com/watch?v=eoix2qjFgDo&feature=emb_logo.

Nelson, Davia, and Nikki Silva. 2018. "'Savior Of Film,' Henri Langlois, Began Extensive Cinema Archive in His Bathtub." Episode. *Morning Edition,* NPR, September 20, 2018.

Obrist, Hans Ulrich. 2014. "Hans Ulrich Obrist: The Art of Curation." An interview by Stuart Jeffries and Nancy Groves. *The Guardian,* Guardian News and Media, March 23, 2014. https://www.theguardian.com/artanddesign/2014/mar/23/hans-ulrich-obrist-art-curator.

The Outlet Dance Project. Accessed March 3, 2021. https://www.theoutletdanceproject.com/.

Payri, Blas. 2018. "Life and Death of Screendance Festivals: A Panorama." *Videodance Studies.*

Pearce, Sheldon, Cassidy George, and Jia Tolentino. 2020. "The Whitewashing of Black Music on TikTok." *The New Yorker.* September 9, 2020. https://www.newyorker.com/culture/cultural-comment/the-whitewashing-of-black-music-on-tiktok.

Petrie, Duncan. 2014. Essay. In *The Emergence of Film Culture: Knowledge Production, Institution Building and the Fate of the Avant-Garde in Europe, 1919–1945,* edited by Malte Hagener, 268–82. New York ; Oxford: Berghahn.

RiverRun International Film Festival. n.d. "History." Accessed March 1, 2021. https://riverrunfilm.com/history/.

Rosenberg, Doug. 2007. Opensource Videodance Symposium, 15–19 June 2006. Findhorn, Scotland. Published by Goat Media.

Rosenblatt, Lauren. 2017. "For Minority Artists in Pittsburgh, Race Plays a Factor in the Hunt for Funding." PublicSource. January 10, 2017. https://www.publicsource.org/for-minority-artists-in-pittsburgh-race-plays-a-factor-in-the-hunt-for-funding/.

Russolo, Luigi. 1913. *The Art of Noise.* Luigi Russolo.

San Francisco Dance Film Festival. "2019 Film Festival Programs." Accessed January 11, 2021. https://www.sfdancefilmfest.org/2019-film-festival-program/.

Sans Souci. Accessed March 2, 2021. http://www.sanssouci.org/.

Schatz, Thomas Gerard. 1989. *The Genius of the System: Hollywood Filmmaking in the Studio Era.* London: Simon & Schuster.

Seibert, Brian. 2018. "The Next Wave of Dance Films, Made on Your Phone, is Here." *The New York Times.* July 31, 2018. https://www.nytimes.com/2018/07/31/arts/dance/mobile-film-festival.html.

Shah, Haleema. 2018. "Inventor, Photographer … Murderer." Broadcast. *Sidedoor* 3, no. 10. Smithsonian, December 12, 2018.

Shevey, Sandra. 2017. "Sandra Shevey Interviews Shirley Clarke." YouTube. August 22, 2017. https://www.youtube.com/watch?v=BKdXthAUIVA.

Sterling, Bruce. 2016. "Hugo Ball's Dada Manifesto, July 1916." *Wired,* 11 July. https://www.wired.com/beyond-the-beyond/2016/07/hugo-balls-dada-manifesto-july-2016/.

Thomas, Jeanne. 1971. "The Decay of the Motion Picture Patents Company." *Cinema Journal* 10, no. 2: 34–40. https://doi.org/https://doi.org/10.2307/1225236.

Turvey, Malcolm. 2003. "Dada between Heaven and Hell: Abstraction and Universal Language in the Rhythm Films of Hans Richter." *October,* vol. 105, pp. 13–36. https://doi.org/10.1162/016228703769684146.

Universal Pictures. "About." https://www.universalpictures.com/about.

Welky, David. 2017. "A World Film Fight: Behind the Scenes with Hollywood and Fascist Italy." *Film and History* 47, no. 1: 4–17. https://doi.org/muse.jhu.edu/article/668275.

Whatley, Sarah. 2010. "The Spectacle of Difference: Dance and Disability on Screen." *The International Journal of Screendance* 1. https://doi.org/10.18061/ijsd.v1i0.6144.

Wild, Jennifer. 2005. "An Artist's Hands: Stella Simon, Modernist Synthesis, and Narrative Resistance." *Framework: The Journal of Cinema and Media* 46, no. 1 (March): 93–105. https://doi.org/https://www.jstor.org/stable/41552429.

Bibliography

Wong, Cindy H. 2011. "History, Structure, and Practice in the Festival World." Essay. In *Film Festivals: Culture, People, and Power on the Global Screen*, 29–64. New Brunswick, NJ: Rutgers University Press.

Interviews

Bernier, Michelle and David Lesserman: June 27, 2018
Bromberg, Ellen: September 14, 2018
Chambers, David: November 17, 2018
Chapman, Andrew: June 27, 2018
Christa, Gabri: November 2, 2018
Cole, Kathryn: July 10, 2017 and June 27, 2018
Cooper, John: October 4, 2018
Elgart, Sarah: August 21, 2018
Flannery, Judy: July 17, 2017
Greene, Brighid: June 26, 2018
Hargraves, Kelly: August 20, 2018
Irons, Kingsley: November 21, 2017
Monroy, Ximena: August 27, 2018
Robideaux, Ann and Donia Salem Harhoor: August 27, 2018
Rosenberg, Douglas: June 26, 2018
Schoenberg, Greta: July 19, 2019
Scully-Thurston, Jennifer: October 20, 2019
Sheppard, Renata: June 25, 2018
Szperling, Silvina: August 28, 2018
Towers, Deirdre: September 23, 2018
Wolff, Liz: August 31, 2017 and June 18, 2018

Index

Academy of Motion Picture Arts and Sciences 31

ADF's Movies by Movers 2, 9, 87–90, 109–112, 121–143, 146, 150, 152–153, 155, 157–163, 165–166, 168

Advance 102

Agite y Sirve Festival 79

Ailey, Alvin 51–52, 98

Alive from Off Center 41, 58

All-Union State Institute of Cinematography 30

American Dance Festival 2, 8, 37, 56, 59, 90, 98, 112, 158

American Guild of Musical Artists 55

American Movie Classics 3

American Straight Photography 28

a/perture 89

Arakelyan, Yulia 152

Are You Holding Me, or Am I Holding Myself? 146

L'Arrivée d'un Train en Gare de la Ciotat 18

Art in Cinema Series 51

Astaire, Fred 3

Atlas, Charles 100

Baer, Ana 60, 62, 175

Ball, Hugo 25

Balla, Giacomo 23

Bandy, Miklos 28

Battery Plum 49–50

Beckford-Smith, Ruth 52

Beenhakker, Hans 54, 188

Ben Hajria, Younes 166

Berkeley, Busby 21

Bernier, Michelle 61, 174–176

Beshir, Jessica 171

Bettis, Valerie 41

Biograph 18–19

Black Ballerina 174

Black Maria Studio 16

Blanco Borelli, Melissa 129, 189

Boundless in Brooklyn 48-Hour Dance Film Contest 74

Bragaglia, Anton Giulio 23

Braun, Susan 46–47, 53–55, 97–98

Breathe In, Breathe Out 7, 149–151

Breen Joseph 21

Brodermann, Cesar 146

Bromberg, Ellen 56–58, 100–101

Brooks, Virginia 98, 188

Bruce 181

Brunius, Jaques 47

Burnett, Marjorie 152–153

Bute, Mary Ellen 29–30

Cabaret Voltaire 24

Cage, John 51

Cannes 32–33, 47, 94, 129

Carmencita 16

Carriage 142

Cave, Mimi 102

Channel 4 41, 58

Chaplin, Charlie 20

Chase, Doris 57, 100, 148

Chiarini, Jamuna 78

Chiti, Remo 23

Choreotones 36–41

Christa, Gabri 66, 104, 170–171

Cine-GUF-Gioventù Universitaría fascista 31

cine-painting 24

Cinecittà 32

Cinémathéque Française 33

Cinematographe 7, 10, 17

Cinépoème 27

Clair, René 25

Clarence White School of Photography 28

Clark, Pat "Veve" 48–49

Clarke, Shirley 35, 100, 180, 188

Clinic of Stumble 51

Co-Laboratory 173–174

Cole, Kat 61, 122, 178–179

Conseil International de la Danse 52

Corra, Bruno 23–24

Cummings, Blondell 180

Cunningham, Merce 75, 100, 188

Cyd Charisse 3

Dada 24–26, 28, 187

Dance Camera West 8, 35, 54, 56–57, 86

Dance:Film Festival 8, 187

195

Index

Dance Film Lab 75–76
Dance Films Association 46–47, 53–54, 96–97, 99, 177–178, 188
Dance Films, Inc. 48
Dance in the Sun 100
Dance Nine 100
Dance Number 22, 180
Dance on Camera Festival 47–48, 53–56, 70–71, 97–99, 169, 176–178
DanceBARN 60, 110, 113
Dancer's Workshop 52
Dances Made to Order 62–64, 80, 122
Dancing on Camera Festival 56, 98
Dare to Dance in Public 67, 75, 80–81, 104
Dash, Julie 180
Dawson, Harry, Jr. 50
DeMarco, Tony 41
Demystavision 52
Deren, Maya 6, 28, 36, 39, 50, 100
Detour Dance 61, 179
Direzione Generale per la Cinematografia 32
Djemille, Fatima 16–17, 187
Dominic, Justin 147
Donen, Stanley 21, 75
Doner, Kitty 36–37, 41
Dreams 4
Duncan, Isadora 46–47, 55
Dunham, Katherine 41

Eastman-Kodak Company 19
Edison, Thomas 15, 55
Edison Trust 19
8½ 3
Elgart, Sarah 67, 75, 80–81, 104
Ellis Won't Be Dancing Today 149
Emak Bakia 27
Emswiller, Ed 50
The Enrichment Center 7, 149
Ente Nationale Industria Cinematographica 21
Entr'act 25
Envisioning Dance on Film and Video 57
Erdos, Rachel 142
Experimental Film Virginia 72

Fairbanks, Douglas 20
Fatima's Coochee-Coochee Dance 16
Fellini, Federico 3–5
Ferguson, Erik 152
Festival for Filmatic Dance 52
The Field 138
Fildes, Simon 59, 187
FilmFest by Rogue Dancer 80
Filming Dance Festival and Symposium 53
Filmstudie 28
Fisher, Katherine Helen 138
Folding Over Twice 7
Font, Nuria 56

42nd Street 3
Fotodianismo 23
Four Women 180
Foursite Film Festival 8
Friedland, Sarah 148
From the Heart of Brahma 146
Funn, Carlos 73, 122
Futurist Manifesto 22

Garafola, Lynn 52
Garcia, Eric 61, 122, 179
Gerasimov Institute 31
Gimp Gait 152–153
Ginanni-Corradini brothers 23, 30
Ginna, Arnaldo 23
Giordano, Gus 98
Glassman, Marc 56
Goddard College 7–8
Grand Café 17
Greene, Brigid 77
Greenfield, Amy 55, 57
Griffith, D.W. 20

Hagan, Mackenzie 7–8
Halprin, Anna 50, 52
Hände: Das Leben Und Die Liebe Eines Zärtlichen Geschlechts 28–29
Harge, Jennifer 74
Hargraves, Kelly 54, 56, 86
Harper, Andrew 164
Hays, Will 20
Hays Agreement 20
Hays Code 20
He Who Dances on Wood 171
Heckroth, Hein 47
Henly, Katherine 164
Hodson, Millicent 48–49, 52–53, 76
Holder, Geoffrey 50
Home Exercises 148
Honsa, Ron 98
Horror Dream 51
Hunter, Brett 7–8
Hybbinette, Pelle 151

Iarisoa, Julie 116–117
In Living Color 3
Indie Grits Film Festival 7, 187
The International Journal of Screendance 59, 124, 129, 133, 144, 170, 188, 189
Intrinsic Moral Evil 145
Irons, Kingsley 62–64, 122

Jackson, Bruce 181
Jacob's Pillow Dance Festival 54
Jones, Bill T. 100

Kappenberg, Claudia 59, 187
Keaton, Buster 20

Index

Keeler, Ruby 3
Kelley, Gene 3
Kerr, Ryan 74
Kessler, Lynette 54, 56
Kidd, Michael 21, 75
Kiesling, Bruce 7
Kinescope 37, 187
Kinesis 25, 49, 51, 76
Kinetic Light 138
Kinetograph 15
Kinetoscope 15–17
Kinetoscope Festival 60
Kiss Me, Kate! 3
Knapp, Amanda 148
Koch, Bryan 62, 64, 122
Koner, Pauline 36–41
Kuntz, Pam 149
Kurosawa, Akira 4

Laemmle, Carl 19–20
Laemmle Film Service 19
La Mostra Cinematograpica di Venezia 31
Lane, Juel D. 136–137
Langlois, Henri 33, 47–48, 53, 187
Lawson, Laurel 138–139
Lello 102
Lenin, Vladimir 30–31
Lenkinski, Ori 142
Lenzu, Anabella 138
Lincoln Center (Puerto Ricans Vs. NYC) 50
Lincoln Square Renewal Project 50
The Little Colonel 3
Little White Salmon Indian Settlement 50
Livingston, Daniel 46
Lopez, Jennifer 3
Luahine, Iolani 50
Luddy, Tom 50
Lumiere, Auguste 17
Lumiere, Louis 17

MA 138
The Maestro 136–137
Maldonado, Edson 172
Månsson, Madeleine 151
Marinetti, Filippo Tommaso 21–24, 181
Markova, Alicia 54
Marks, Victoria 100–101
McElroy, Frances 174
McPherson, Katrina 59
Meade, Elizabeth 116
Meerson, Mary 47, 187
Meeting Place 148
Meliés, Georges 55
Merce by Merce by Paik Part One: Blue Studio 100
A Meta-Kinesis Preserve: And We Went Dancing in the Electronic Mirror 51
Metro-Goldwyn-Meyer 20

Michael, Leen 146
Miller, Anne 3
Miller, Grant 152
Miller, Virginia 41
Mitoma, Judy 57
Modern Daydreams: Part One 102
Monroe, Raquel 129, 189
Monroy, Ximena 79
Moreno, Rita 3
Moser, Jocelyn 116
Mostra de Videodansa de Barcelona 56
Motion Picture Patents Company 119
Motion Picture Producers and Distributors Association 20
Movies by Movers 2, 9, 87, 89, 90, 121, 124–125, 129, 146, 150, 157
Moving 24 FPS 73–74, 122, 188
Moving Body—Moving Image 66, 69, 104, 170–171
Moving Pictures Festival 56
Murnane, Bridget 100
Mussolini, Benito 20–22, 31–32
Muybridge, Eadweard 14–16

Namath, Ted 29
Nelson, Fred 171
New York Dance Film Society 46
New York Moment 164
Nickolais, Alwin 51
The Nicholas Brothers 3, 5
Nilsson, Peder 151
No More Beautiful Dances 138
Noble, Duncan 39–41
Notes from There (Notas Desde Allá) 145
Novissima-Film 23

of bones || hollye bynum 74
Off, Carl 146
Ok, Prumsodun 145–146
Olympia 32
Opensource 59
Ortiz, Raphael Montañez 180
Ostersmith, Suzanne 117
O'Toole, Deirdre 73
The Outlet Dance Project 78, 122, 156–163, 168, 189
Oved, Margalit 50
Oviasu, Esosa 172

Pacific Film Archives 50
Paramount Picture Corporation 20
passages from James Joyce's *Finnegan's Wake* 30
Pathé 19
Payri, Blas 83, 188
Perez Navarro, Cinthia 116–117
phonograph 15
Pickaninny Dance 16

197

Pickford, Mary 20
Plumb, Glenn E. 48
Premiere Festival International Du Film De Danse 48
Prim, Ann 145
Production Code Administration 21

Rastus, Joe 180
Ray, Man 27
Redford, Robert 75
Revel in Your Body 138
Rhythm in Light 29
Rhythmus 25
Richter, Hans 25–28, 30
Riefenstahl, Leni 32
River Run International Film Festival 4, 9
RKO Radio Pictures Incorporated 20
The Road to Ose Tura (A Prayer Ain't a Prayer Unless You Say It Out Loud) 136
Robbins, Jerome 20, 188
Robert Jeoffrey Ballet 51
Robideaux, Ann 78, 122, 161
Robinson, Bill "Bojangles" 3
Rogers, Ginger 3
Rose, Mitchell 57, 102
Rosenberg, Douglas 8, 56, 58–59, 98–100, 187
Rousseve, David 172
Rowlson-Hall, Celia 138

St. Denis, Ruth 55, 98
Salem Harhoor, Donia 78, 122, 157, 161
Sampson, Efeya 136
San Francisco Ballet 52, 174
San Francisco Dance Film Festival 51–52, 102–103, 121, 169, 172–174, 188
Sans Souci Festival of Dance Cinema 60–62, 110, 174–176
Schneemann, Carolee 140
Schonberg, Greta 102
Scorsese, Martin 4
Screendance Educators Symposium 56–57
Scully-Thurston, Jennifer 80–81, 105
Sergel, Ruth 181
Serpentine Dance 18
Settimelli, Emilio 23
Shake the Dust 173
Shawn, Ted 55
Sheppard, Alice 138–139
Sheppard, Renata 72–73, 188
Simon, Stella F. 28–29
Sioux Ghost Dance 16
Skånes Dansteater 151
Sloan, Lenwood 51–52, 121
Smith, Kathleen 56
Smuin, Michael 52
Society for Patakinetics 48, 50
A Soft Place to Land 102
Sokolow, Anna 50, 100

Soufisme 166
Southeastern Center for Contemporary Art 89
Le Squelette Joyeux 18
Stanford, Leland 14
Stauffacher, Frank 51
Stormy Weather 3, 5
A Study of Choreography for the Camera 39
Sundance 75–76
Superfest 153
Susilowati, Sr.i 172
Swanson, Gloria 20
Swing Time 3
Szpirling, Silvina 56–58

Teatro Experimentale de Cali 50
Technische Hochschule 28
Temple, Shirley 3
Thaïs 23
This Black 171
Thompkins, Cameron 172
Tiny Dance Film Festival 61, 178–179
Tolliver, Denny 180
Towers, Deirdre 53–54, 98, 187–188
A Trip Around My Navel 116
Turchin Center for the Visual Arts 112–113
Turner Classic Movies 3
20th Century–Fox 20
Two Seconds After Laughter 172
Tzara, Tristan 25

Ulrich Obrist, Hans 85, 96
UMove Online Videodance Festival 80
Unapologetic Me: BLACK|GAY|MAN 147
United Artists 20
Universal City 19
Universal Pictures 19–20
University of North Carolina School of the Arts 3
Utah International Screendance Festival 56, 58, 100–101

Vanderbeek, Stan 50
Van Tuyl, Marian 51
Vera-Ellen 3
VideoDanzaBA 56–57
A Visual Diary 180
Vitagraph 18
Vormittagsspuk 26–27
Voulkos, Peter 49

Waking the Green Sound: A Dance Film for the Trees 152
Warner Brothers 20
Waters, Sylvia 52
Weistra, Harm 145
West Side Story 3, 20
"What Happened to My Legs" 116

Index

White, Marcus 73, 133
White Christmas 3
Wilder, Holly 138
Wilkins, Walter 180
Winter, Pioneer 152–153
Wise, Robert 20
Wobbly Dance 152
World War II 21, 26, 32–33, 36

World's Columbian Exposition 16
Wrecked Pulse 151

Young, Linda Martina 180
Your Approval Is Not Essential 146

zoopraxiscope 15